THE PEDANT IN THE KITCHEN

THE PEDANT

IN THE KITCHEN

JULIAN BARNES

Atlantic Books
London

*The***Guardian**

www.julianbarnes.com

First published in Great Britain in 2003 by Atlantic Books,
on behalf of Guardian Newspapers Ltd.
Atlantic Books is an imprint of Grove Atlantic Ltd.

10 9 8 7 6 5 4 3 2 1

A CIP record for this book is available from the British Library

ISBN 1 84354 239 0

Designed by Richard Marston
Illustrations by Joe Berger
Printed in Great Britain by CPI Glasgow

Grove Atlantic Ltd
Ormond House
26–27 Boswell Street
London
WC1N 3JZ

to She For Whom

CONTENTS

A LATE-ONSET COOK

I am a late-onset cook. In my childhood, the usual genteel protectionism surrounded activities in the voting booth, the marital bed, and the pew. I failed to notice a fourth secret place – secret, at least, from boys – in the English middle-class home: the kitchen. Meals and my mother emerged from it – meals often based on my father's garden produce – but neither he, my brother, nor I enquired, or were encouraged to enquire, about the transformational process. No one went so far as to say that cooking was sissy, it was just something that domestic males weren't suited to. On school mornings my father would prepare breakfast – re-heated porridge with golden syrup, bacon, toast – while his sons applied them-selves to shoe-cleaning and kitchen-stove duty: rake out the ashes, refill with coke.

But male culinary competence was clearly limited to such matutinal dabbling. This was made plain one time when my mother was called away. My father prepared my packed lunch and, not understanding the theory of the sandwich, lovingly inserted extra items that he knew I especially liked. A few hours later, on a Southern Region train to an out-of-town sports field, I opened my lunch bag in front of fellow rugby players. My sandwiches were sodden, falling to bits, and bright red from the paternally cut beetroot; they blushed for me as I blushed for their contriver.

And as with sex, politics, and religion, so with cooking; by the time I began finding out about it for myself, it was too late to ask my parents. They had failed to instruct me, and I would punish them by not asking now. I was in my mid-twenties and reading for the bar; some of the food I concocted at that time was criminal. Top of my range was bacon chop, peas, and potatoes. The peas were frozen, of course; the potatoes were tinned, pre-peeled, and came in a sweetish brine I liked to drink; the bacon chop was unlike anything subsequently encountered under that name. Boneless, pre-shaped, and of a luminous pink, it was distinguished by its ability to keep a fluorescent hue however long you cooked it. This gave much latitude to the chef: it wasn't undercooked unless positively cold, or overcooked unless coal-black and alight. Then butter was lavished on the peas, the potatoes, and, usually, the chop as well.

The key factors governing my 'cooking' at this time were poverty, lack of skill, and gastronomic conservatism. Others might have lived on offal; tinned tongue was as near as I would go to that, though corned beef doubtless contained body parts that would have been unwelcome in their original form. One staple was breast of lamb: easy to roast, fairly easy to see when it was done, large enough to yield three successive dinners for about a shilling. Then I graduated to shoulder of lamb. With this I would serve an enormous leek, carrot and potato pie made from a recipe in the London Evening Standard. The pie's cheese sauce always tasted strongly of flour, though this gradually diminished with daily re-heating. Only later did I work out why.

My repertoire broadened. Meat and vegetables were the main things to be, if not mastered, at least somewhat tamed. Then came puddings and the odd soup; later – much later – gratins, pasta, risotto, soufflés. Fish was always a problem, and is still only half-solved.

On home visits, it emerged that I cooked. My father observed this development with the mild, liberal suspicion previously deployed when I was spotted reading *The Communist Manifesto* or when I forced him to listen to Bartók string quartets. If this is as bad as it gets, his attitude seemed to imply, then I can probably handle it. My mother was happier; daughterless, she at least had one child who retrospectively appreciated her years in the galley. Not that we sat around swapping recipes; but she noted the covetous eye I now laid on her ancient copy of *Mrs Beeton*. My brother, shielded by collegiate life and marriage, didn't cook anything beyond a fried egg until his fifties.

The result of all this – and I doggedly blame the 'all this' rather than myself – is that while I now cook with enthusiasm and pleasure, I do so with little sense of freedom or imagination. I need an exact shopping list and an avuncular cookbook. The ideal of carefree marketing – waltzing off with wicker basket over the arm, relaxedly buying what the day has best to offer, and then contriving it into something which might or might not have been made before – will always be beyond me.

In the kitchen I am an anxious pedant. I adhere to gas marks and cooking times. I trust instruments rather than myself. I doubt I shall ever test whether a chunk of meat is done by prodding it with my forefinger. The only liberty I

take with a recipe is to increase the quantity of an ingredient of which I particularly approve. That this is not an infallible precept was confirmed by an epically filthy dish I once made involving mackerel, Martini and breadcrumbs: the guests were more drunk than sated.

I am also a reluctant taster, with excuses always at the ready. For instance: it can't possibly taste the same now, in the afternoon, with remnants of sweet tea in the mouth, as it will and should this evening, after a morale-boosting gin and tonic. What this means is: I'm scared to discover how unlike actual food it tastes at this stage. The other reliable get-out is to tell yourself there is no point in tasting because you're following the recipe to the letter, and since (a) the recipe doesn't insist upon your tasting at this point, and (b) it's by a respected authority, how could things possibly end up other than they should?

This is, I realize, somewhat less than mature. So too are my infantile bouts of cheffish volatility. If you were in my kitchen, idly stuck your finger into something and said that it tasted good, I would get the hump because I'd been looking forward to surprising you with it on the plate. And if, on the other hand, you were mildly, generously, and civilly to suggest a touch more nutmeg might help, or the sauce could just possibly do with further reduction, I would regard this as the grossest interference.

My wrath is also frequently turned against the cookbooks on which I rely so heavily. Still, this is one area where pedantry is both understandable and important: and the self-taught, anxious, page-scowling domestic cook is about as pedantic as you can get. But then, why should a cookbook be less precise than a manual of surgery? (Always assuming, as one nervously does, that manuals of surgery are indeed precise. Perhaps some of them sound just like cookbooks: 'Sling a gout of anaesthetic down the tube, hack a chunk off the patient, watch the blood drizzle, have a beer with your mates, sew up the cavity...') Why should a word in a recipe be less important than a word in a novel? One can lead to physical indigestion, the other to mental.

I sometimes wish it were all different; most late-onset cooks do. If only my mother had taught me to boil and bake all those years ago ... Apart from anything else, I wouldn't be so pathetically needy of praise nowadays. As the front door closes on the last departing guest, I feel a habitual whine rising to my lips: 'I overdid the lamb/beef/whatever.' By which I mean: 'I didn't, did I, and if I did it doesn't matter, does it?' Mostly I get the contradiction I crave; occasionally a reminder of the house rule that after the age of twenty-five you aren't allowed to blame your parents for anything. Indeed, you're even allowed to forgive them. So, OK, Dad, those beetroot sandwiches: you know, they were fine, quite tasty, and – well – really original. I couldn't have made them better myself.

WARNING: PEDANT AT WORK

In my early thirties, when the kitchen was slowly mutating from a place of resented necessity to one of tense pleasure, I had my first attempt at Vichy carrots. Naturally, I looked up a recipe in a book – one written, as it happened, by a friend of She For Whom the Pedant Cooks. Carrots, water, salt, sugar, butter, pepper, parsley: nothing too challenging about these ingredients. I approached their assembly with something close to real confidence. I even had time to wonder whether it was Vichy as in Pétain (the ingredients seen as collaborators) or Vichy as in health and spa (though what about all the butter, sugar, and salt?) or merely Vichy as in a long-established recipe from those parts.

Even to one preternaturally alert to potential hazards, the recipe looked a breeze. Basically: peel, slice, boil, season,

worry a bit about sticking and burning. I was about to hurl myself into it when I noticed something wrong with the text. It was laid out in three sections, but the sections themselves were numbered 1, 2, and 4. I showed it to She For Whom, who was equally baffled by the missing segue. She suggested ringing up the cook; it was, after all, her book.

I didn't think I could do that. Doctors dread that moment when a gregarious meal is spoilt by their neighbour starting to roll up his trouser leg with a murmur of 'I wonder if you'd mind taking a look at this. . . ?' Novelists dread the moment when a friendly face suddenly turns out to have written a short story – not too long, only 130 pages – about which their opinion would be truly valued. Similarly, cookbook writers must dread the phone call – always just as they're at work on their own dinner – referring them to some obscure problem in a volume now well out of print; or asking if, since there don't seem to be any powdered porcupine quills in the larder, it would matter if. . .

Still, with guests on the way, I nerved myself and made the call. I outlined the problem.

'Read me the recipe,' said the cook. I did so. 'That sounds all right,' she replied.

'No, the point is,' I replied pedantically, 'the point is

whether there's a stage 3 which has been missed out by the publishers, in which case what is it? – or whether the 4 is a misprint for 3.'

'Read it again,' she said (no doubt whisking up a sea-urchin soufflé while shoulder-propping the phone). I did so. 'That sounds all right,' she repeated, clearly rather baffled by my call.

It was at this moment that I grasped the serious divide between Us and Them. If the rich are different because they have more money, so cooks whose recipes we follow are different because they no longer need the advice we so anxiously require. Being a great cook is one thing; being a decent cookery writer is quite another, and is based – like novel-writing – on imaginative sympathy and precise descriptive powers. Contrary to sentimental belief, most people don't have a novel inside them; nor do most chefs have a cookbook.

'Artists should have their tongues cut out,' Matisse once said, and the same – if even more metaphorically – applies to many chefs. They should be chained to their stoves and merely allowed to pass food through the hatch as we require it. I once stayed two nights at the Hôtel du Midi in Lamastre, famously praised by Elizabeth David, and which continues to serve the finest *ancienne cuisine*. As I was checking out, I noticed a poster of the Ardèche's top twenty chefs. They were pictured standing cheerily on the steps of a chateau, all primped and toqued. I asked Madame which one was her husband.

'Surely you recognize him?' she asked. No. In two days I hadn't set eyes on him. 'Ah, that's because he's always in the kitchen.' Only later did I reflect how rare – and wise – this was.

Of course we want recipes, and we have every right to them. In the old days the transmission would have been oral and matrilineal. Then it became written and increasingly patriarchal. Nowadays we can be taught by either sex and the method may be oral (the TV chef), written (the cookbook) or both at the same time (the TV tie-in cookbook). I remain a text-based cook and am broadly suspicious of those persuaded to inflate their personalities in front of the camera. Even in the early days, TV cooks were hardly instruments of Reithian high purpose: look at Fanny and Johnny Craddock. Today, it is even more chummy and collusive: 'Hey, look, any mutt can fling one of these together – don't think you have to be anyone special or posh or clever.'

No, of course you don't. But learning and teaching, however much we turn them into face-painted fun, are still learning and teaching. When I was a schoolboy, we used to jeer, 'Those who can, do; those who can't, teach.' To which my father, an ironical man who was also a schoolmaster, used to add the rider: 'And those who can't teach, teach teachers.' The jeer, I notice, has now been craftily re-appropriated by the teaching profession, which advertises with the slogan 'Those who can, teach.'

Those who can, cook; those who can't, wash up. And while we're about it: pedantry and non-pedantry are indicators only of temperament, not of culinary skill. Non-pedants frequently misunderstand pedants and are inclined to adopt an air of superiority. 'Oh, I don't follow recipes,' they will say, as if cooking from a text were like making love with a sex-manual open at your elbow. Or: 'I read recipes, but only to get ideas.' Well, fine, but let me ask you this: would you use a lawyer who said 'Oh, I glance at a few statutes, but only to get ideas'? One of the best cooks I know automatically gets down the recipe book whenever she roasts a chicken. The truth is, pedantry and non-pedantry can cut both ways. A pedant may vary from a dogged, uninquisitive, cloth-palated follower of orders to a devotee bent on doing everything absolutely right; while a non-pedant might be a simple lazy-bones or someone airy-fairily 'creative' in the worst, self-applauding way, or someone of justified confidence who has mastered technique and heard all the secret harmonies of the kitchen. I don't necessarily prefer being cooked for by a pedant; but I do have deep fellow-feeling for what is going on around the stove and inside the head. And I would include all the higher levels of the profession in my camp too. Chefs may be as experimental and inventive as you like (though much apparent originality turns out to be mere theft), but they know that a dish, in order to be the dish they are proud to serve, must be created in a very, very precise way, with the smallest latitude for error. 'Oh, that'll do' is not a phrase often heard in top restaurant kitchens. The worst meal I've ever eaten – worst in the sense of most resented – was at a starry French restaurant where the chef had raised non-pedantry into a principle and a slogan: he advertised what he did as *cuisine d'instinct*. The first and only night I ate *chez lui*, his instinct was to bail out single-handedly the nation's entire vinegar industry. Course after course was served in a soup-plate ankle-deep in vinegar, until you began to dread what cruelties were going to be wrought on the cheese, the crème brûlée, and the coffee.

Twenty years on, I still cook Vichy carrots from the same recipe, and have more or less decided that stage 3, whether it exists or not, is probably irrelevant. And at some point I found out why they are called Vichy carrots: because they were originally cooked in spa water. The accepted substitute – before bottled water became as ubiquitous as it is – used to be a pinch of bicarb in tap water. However, as the infinitely wise Jane Grigson notes: 'I should be surprised if you would know the difference between glazed carrots cooked with Vichy water or tap water plus bicarb or tap water on its own.' Now that's the sort of sentence I like.

TAKE TWO
MEDIUM ONIONS

The neighbour of the mother of a friend of mine (yes I know, but it happens to be true) decided to make some jam. She had never made jam before. My friend's mother advised blackberry and apple. The next day, the neighbour came round with the grim result: an inch or two of black, solidified matter, which might possibly yield to a dentist's drill, squatting at the bottom of a pot. Something had gone wrong, she thought.

Under cross examination from the recipe police, she admitted she had looked up a book in which it said: 'One pound of fruit to one pound sugar.' For some reason (like being a bear of small brain) she convinced herself that the best way to measure the ingredients was to use an empty jam jar that had once contained a pound of commercial jam. She filled it once with fruit for the pound of fruit, and once with sugar for the pound of sugar.

I think we're allowed more than a laugh at this; perhaps even a smug chortle. We've all done some pretty risible things in our time – I know a Canadian novelist who once tried to make pesto from dried basil – but nothing quite as risible as this. And at such times, you have to feel sorry for cookbook writers. They construct their best recipes, they get friends to road-test them, the publishers' editors add their tablespoonful, and then – something like this happens. It must be the stuff of after-dinner speeches at culinary conferences; it might even be a TV series, after *The World's Worst Drivers* and *Neighbours from Hell*. If only they'd done what we said. . .

The Pedant in the Kitchen is not concerned with whether cooking is a science or an art; he will settle for it being a craft, like woodwork or home welding. Nor is he a competitive cook. It surprised him to discover that gardening, for all its air of prelapsarian serenity, is furiously competitive, frequently indulged in by the envious, the deceitful, the quietly criminal. Doubtless there are competitive cooks, but the Pedant is not one of them. He just wants to cook tasty, nutritious food; he just wants not to poison his friends; he just wants slowly to expand his repertoire.

Ah, the pathos of those 'just's. With these craftsman's ambitions, he is never going to invent his own dishes. He might occasionally engage in some minor act of disobedience; but he is, in essence, a recipe-bound drudge, a careful follower of the words of others. Thus is the Pedant ever bound to the rock of his Pedantry: not where he eats liver, but where his liver is eaten.

The Pedant approaches a new recipe, however straightforward, with old anxieties: words flash at him like stop signs. Is this recipe framed in this imprecise way because there is a happy latitude – or rather, a scary freedom – for interpretation; or because the writer isn't capable of expressing him or herself more accurately? It starts with simple words. How big is a 'lump', how voluminous is a 'slug' or a 'gout', when does a 'drizzle' become rain? Is a 'cup' a rough-and-ready generic term or a precise American measure? Why tell us to add a 'wineglass' of something, when wineglasses come in so many sizes? Or – to return briefly to jam – how about this instruction from Richard Olney: 'Throw in as many strawberries as you can hold piled up in joined hands.' I mean, really. Are we meant to write to the late Mr Olney's executors

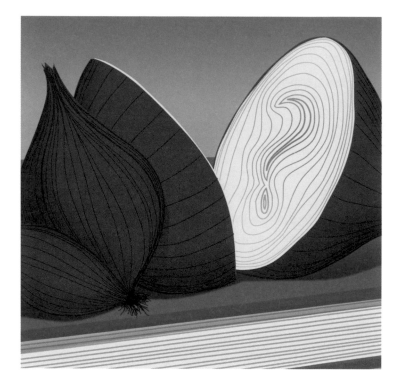

and ask how big his hands were? What if children made this jam, or circus giants?

Let's take the problem of the onion. I shan't enter the absorbing debate – a recent long-runner among correspondents to the *Guardian* – over how to peel one without blubbing, except to warn you that if, as I once did, you try wearing a pair of strimmer's goggles, the plastic lens will quickly steam up and there will be much blood on the chopping board. No, the problems are these.

(1) For recipe writers, onions come in only three sizes, 'small', 'medium', and 'large', whereas onions in your shopping bag vary from the size of a shallot to that of a curling stone. So an instruction such as 'Take two medium onions' sets off a lot of pedantic scrabbling in the onion basket for bulbs that fit the description (obviously, since medium is a comparative term, you have to compare across the whole spectrum of onions you possess).

(2) The applicable verbs are generally 'slice' and 'chop', which I logically assume always to indicate different actions: 'slice' meaning cut across a halved onion, resulting in a clutter of semi-circles; 'chop' involving preliminary lengthwise incisions from tip to root in the halved bulb, resulting in a mound of smaller bits. 'Slice' may be qualified by 'finely';

'chop' by both 'finely' and 'roughly'. So that comes to five methods to decide among and delay the knife. Of course, if you ask yourself the sensible reverse question – have you ever served or been served a dish in which you judged that the onions could or should have been cut differently? – the answer is, of course, never. But the Pedant will conclude from this, not that dismembering onions is a no-fail activity, but that so far everything has worked out OK only because everyone has been diligently following instructions.

This all explains why I never attend to the estimated preparation times that some recipes helpfully include. Even if generously based on a multiple of what a professional cook might take, they are always over-optimistic. Cookbook writers, it seems to me, fail to imagine the time a punter takes holding up a trembling tablespoon and wondering if its piled contents are better described as 'rounded' or 'heaped'; or glossing the word 'surplus' in an instruction like 'trim off the surplus fat'. I recently found myself contemplating the line 'soak the beans overnight or while you work' and seriously wondering if there were an implication that one option might be better: could the writer be hinting that the nocturnal, undisturbed pulse might fatten up better than one exposed to the light and noise of the day?

Much more useful than notional and guilt-inducing preparation times are indications of holding points, i.e. the stage at which you can stop cooking, shove the whole thing in the fridge, and take a break. Despite empirical evidence that there are many dishes which are unharmed by re-heating, this is a prejudice difficult to shift. It was Marcella Hazan in her *Classic Italian Cookbook* who for me first spoke the liberating words: 'You may complete the dish up to step 6 several hours in advance.' And then, even better, 'The dish can be cooked entirely in advance several days ahead.'

What we need liberating from, more broadly, is what might be called the restaurant fallacy. We go out to eat, have three courses that arrive more or less as the stomach craves them, and the whole conspiracy of the place invites us to conclude that the food has been prepared from scratch, especially for us, in the mere time since we gave our order: a helping of beans put on to boil, a few potatoes shoved in the oven to roast, a little Béarnaise whisked up, and so on. And the same for everyone else in the restaurant. We know this is utterly foolish, yet part of us continues to believe it, and the effect when we first start to cook for others is maleficent. We imagine that everything must be done in one culinary swoop, culminating a few seconds before the meal is served. But even if that were possible (which it isn't), we forget that in any case we are not just the chef; we are also meant to be the waiter, maître d, cloakroom attendant, and sparkling fellow-guest.

Kitchen shops sell a lot of useful gadgets and time-saving equipment. One of the most useful and most liberating would be a sign that the domestic cook could place to catch the eye in moments of tension: THIS IS NOT A RESTAURANT.

BY THE BOOK

How many cookbooks do you have?

  (a) Not enough

  (b) Just the right number

  (c) Too many?

If you answered (b) you are disqualified for lying or compla-
cency or not being interested in food or (scariest of all)
having worked out everything perfectly. You score points for
(a) and also for (c), but to score maximum points you need
to have answered (a) *and* (c) in equal measure. (a) because
there is always something new to be learned, someone
coming along to make it all clearer, easier, more foolproof,
more authentic; (c) because of the regular mistakes made
when applying (a).

The main, easily accessible shelf in our kitchen holds

twenty-four books; the two higher shelves, thirty-four; the shelf in the hole where the washing-machine lives contains an immediate back-up of twenty books; there are six in the lavatory, and I would guess another ten to fifteen scattered round the house. Nearly a hundred, let's say. Is this

(a) Modest

(b) Just right

(c) Obscenely large?

As before, the correct answer is (a) plus (c). Every so often, in an attempt to reduce (c) to (b), a cull takes place, and evidence of various unfulfilled culinary ambitions (a surprisingly high proportion of them relating to stir-fry) will be Oxfammed.

The next cull, for instance, will have to consider Nigel Slater's juice book, *Thirst*, which I bought a few months ago. Nothing wrong with the book, I'm sure. The main problem is, we don't have a juicer. It's not that I haven't tried. I once read a newspaper survey of rival machines and sent off a cheque to someone who proved a fly-by-night merchant. Why did I believe that a firm with apparently green credentials must necessarily be honest? (The cheque was my mistake, the newspaper's ombudswoman explained: if I'd paid by credit card I wouldn't have lost out. She also told me, in

passing, that I could have bought just as good a juicer for half the price – which didn't make me feel any better either.)

So: a juice book but no juicer. The logic points to Oxfam. On the other hand, this could be the year of a successful juicer purchase; and it's a very attractively produced book with a citrus-coloured, rubberized binding you can sponge down when you squirt all over it. Though I suppose you're more likely to squirt all over the open pages, which aren't rubberized – maybe they should have been, like that c. 1900 Paris newspaper printed on vulcanized paper so that the languorous *boulevardier* could read it in the bath. . . Oh, all right then, keep *Thirst*, at least until the cull after next.

If you're just starting up the vertiginous curve of cookbook ownership, allow me to offer certain words of advice, all of it paid for in money.

(1) Never buy a book because of its pictures. Never, ever, point at a photo in a cookbook and say, 'I'm going to make that.' You can't. I once knew a commercial photographer who specialized in food and, believe me, the post-production work that recently gave us a slimline Kate Winslet is as nothing compared to what they shamelessly do to food.

(2) Never buy books with tricksy layouts: for instance, one with each page sliced horizontally into three, so that in

theory you can summon up a near-infinite array of three-course meals without having to keep flicking back and forth.

(3) Avoid books with too wide a compass – anything remotely called *Great Dishes of the World* – or too narrow a one: *Sargasso Seafood* or *Waffle Wonderment*.

(4) Never buy the chef's recipe book on pointed display as you leave a restaurant. Remember: that's why you went to the restaurant in the first place – to eat their cooking, not your own feebler version of it.

(5) Never buy a juice book if you haven't a juicer.

(6) Resist, if possible, attractive anthologies of regional recipes, which you are tempted to buy as souvenirs of foreign holidays. I proved this rule with the *ne plus ultra* of cookbooks, one devoted to Cantal cuisine. It hogged space for years, constantly evading the cull on sentimental grounds, and I never cooked from it once. Cantal food tastes best in the Cantal, where it rains a lot and there is no other choice of cuisine. How many different ways of cooking stuffed cabbage do you need?

(7) Avoid books of famous recipes from the past, especially if reproduced in facsimile edition with period woodcuts.

(8) Never replace your tatty old Jane Grigson or Elizabeth

David with a new version containing exactly the same text, even if it does now have pictures (*see* 1). You will never use it and will go back to the original tatty paperback because it has your marginal notes and you rightly feel comfortable with it.

(9) Never buy a collection of recipes put together for charity, especially one with TV newsreaders offering the secret of their favourite dish. Just give the cover price direct to the charity: that way, they will get more, and you won't have to cull next time round.

(10) Remember that cookery writers are no different from other writers: many have only one book in them (and some shouldn't have let it out in the first place). Consider this possibility when the new one is being puffed.

Regular culling – as much as specific purchase – will leave you in the end with a core kitchen library suited to your taste buds, skill-level, ambition and pocket. Over the years, mine has ended up being built around the following: one encyclopaedia (Alan Davidson's immense *Oxford Companion to Food* having ousted the Larousse), two classic compendia (*The Joy of Cooking* and Constance Spry), two triple-decker coursebooks (Prue Leith and Delia), half a dozen Jane Grigsons, three or four Elizabeth Davids, three

Marcella Hazans, two River Cafes, a couple of Simon Hopkinsons, one Alastair Little, one Richard Olney, one Jocelyn Dimbleby, one Frances Bissell, one Myrtle Allen, one Rowley Leigh.

These are books in regular use; nearby are several dozen in occasional service. Some books I only ever consult for a single recipe: such as Margaret Costa's *Four Seasons Cookery Book* for smoked haddock soufflé or Susan Campbell's *English Cookery New and Old* for autumn pudding (a far superior version of summer pudding, with elderberries, blackberries and crab apples). Why, since these are so trustworthy, don't I try others from the same book? I don't know. Then why not photocopy the one recipe you do use, paste it into your own recipe book and Oxfam the original? Maybe because a continuing loyalty to the actual page on which the recipe was first read somehow prevents this.

Ah yes, your own recipe book. You will need some kind of small scrapbook or filing system for all those newspaper and magazine cuttings. Another word of advice: don't stick them in until you've made the dish at least twice and know it has some chance of longevity. Such a cuttings book will, over the years, testify to the strange trajectory of your cooking. It will also bring back moments in the same way as a photograph album: I used to make that? And that really stodgy vegetable pie? And that thingy in filo pastry which used to make me so cross? And didn't I cook this the night when. . . ? You will be surprised by how much emotional and psychological history you might be storing up when you innocently paste in a slightly stained newspaper clipping.

And now I think I'll go out and buy a juicer. So that I won't have to throw out my juice book next time, or next time but one.

THE TEN-MINUTE
MAESTRO

A summer's day in Kent, late morning, many years ago. The heat is rising, the son of the house is practising his tennis serve on windfalls, while his mother, a stylish and ironical woman, sits quietly shelling peas. Guests arrive for lunch; she continues relaxedly pinging peas into a colander, which I find impressive (already, in pre-culinary days, I am exhibiting sympathetic kitchen anxiety). Drinks are served and unhurriedly she rises and wanders back to the house. We are called to lunch and I eat an enormous number of peas from a vast bowl. Later, when I help clear to the kitchen, I spot several empty, barely concealed Birds Eye packets. I mention this to my hostess, who doesn't turn a hair. 'They never notice,' she replies with a smile.

This was my first introduction to humanity's constant

quest to combine the virtues of slow food and fast food. Unknown to me, the most famous attempt had already been published – and by a Frenchman (well, a Polish-Frenchman) at that. *La Cuisine en Dix Minutes ou l'Adaptation au Rhythme moderne* by Edouard de Pomiane came out here in 1948. Had my hostess read it, she might have saved herself even more time:

> *PEAS. Buy cooked peas in a tin. A half-pound tin is sufficient for two or three people. Open the tin. Pour the contents into a bowl. Drain off the liquid. There is always too much.*

There follow three specific recipes, all coming in at well under the ten-minute mark.

I first heard Pomiane's name a few years ago, when a friend passed on his recipe for quick tomato soup: halve tomatoes, whack them in a high oven, liquidize. Some central factor must have been lost in transmission, because when I tried it, a whole oven-trayful of tomatoes produced (in more like six times ten minutes) a small bowl of pippy scarlet detritus, best suited for spreading on toast. Recently I came across a second-hand copy of *Cooking in Ten Minutes*, an attractive book with woodcuts after Toulouse-Lautrec. I checked the recipe for quick tomato soup. It was not at all as I had been told:

Boil three-quarters of a pint of water in a saucepan and stir in a good soup spoonful of tomato extract. Add two dessertspoonfuls of fine semolina, stirring as you do. Salt. Let it boil for six minutes. Add two ounces of thick cream. Serve.

So much for the oral tradition. Anyway, I had a go at this authorized version, and it made a bowl of beautifully pink semolina sludge with some indissoluble lumps in the bottom. It tasted like a vaguely nutritious wallpaper paste. And the more I browsed through the 300 recipes intended 'for the student, for the midinette, for the clerk, for the artist, for lazy people, poets, men of action, dreamers and scientists', the more the book seemed an aromatic trifle very much of its age. The recipe for tomato salad ends: 'In the south of France a clove of finely minced garlic is always added. In a temperate climate, however, this is not recommended.' Not recommended? Times have changed: it isn't all porridge and Brussels sprouts up here in the north any more. And then there was Monsieur de P.'s jocose Gallic dedication: 'I dedicate this book to Mme X, asking for ten minutes of her kind attention.' 'Allo 'Allo, sacré bleu, zut alors, and all that.

It was at this point that I read Elizabeth David's two essays on the ten-minute maestro in *An Omelette and a Glass of Wine*. She told me that Pomiane (1875–1964) was a food scientist and dietician who taught at the Institut Pasteur for half a century; a contrarian and *provocateur* who found in classic French haute cuisine much that was theoretically and actually indigestible. In E.D.'s incontrovertible opinion, a number of items that the new wave of French chefs in the 1960s and 1970s brought to fame – like Michel Guérard's *confiture d'oignons* – were actually first proposed by Pomiane.

David also quoted a couple of his non-ten-minute recipes. Tomatoes somehow being the theme, I was drawn to *Tomates à la Crème*, which Pomiane learned from his Polish mother, and which, according to E.D., 'taste[s] so startlingly unlike any other dish of cooked tomatoes that any restaurateur who put it on his menu would, in all probability, soon find it listed in the guide books as a regional speciality.' You take six tomatoes, halve them, melt a lump of butter, put the tomatoes in a frying pan cut side down, prick their rounded sides, turn again (to let the juices run out), turn back up at once, add 3 fl oz double cream, mix, let it all bubble, serve.

I didn't much trust this: the quantity of butter was imprecise, the strength of the gas unspecified. Further, it was mid-February, so the best tomatoes I could find were pale orange,

frost-hard, and pretty juice-free inside. I fanatically observed the approximations of Pomiane's recipe, while chucking in a little salt, pepper, and sugar in the tiny hope of not disgracing the kitchen... and the result was unbelievably good – the method had somehow extracted richness from half a dozen fruits which looked as if they had long ago mislaid their essence.

So then it was off to www.abebooks.com for a copy of *Cooking with Pomiane*. You can spot immediately what Elizabeth David saw in him: they both favour the same sort of French cooking (regional, bourgeois, undoctrinaire) and employ a similar layout and succinctness in their recipes. The main difference is in their tone; and this is crucial to a domestic pedant. E.D. is, to say the least, a little unbending. This (from a recipe for Mushrooms in Cream) is about as chatty as she gets: 'My sisters and I had a nanny who used to make these for us over the nursery fire, with mushrooms which we had gathered ourselves in the early morning.' Does it make you feel a touch excluded? Here is Pomiane (New Potatoes with Tarragon): 'I used to fancy myself as a botanist, but my illusions were shattered when I asked a charming young saleswoman for seeds of parsley, chervil and tarragon. "Tarragon does not produce a fertile seed," she replied. "If you want a plant, here you are. In three years it will die. Come back again and see me."'

Pomiane gives you a recipe for deep-fried chunks of calf's head and then, as if sensing your uncertainty, adds, 'Try this, it is really rather good.' He advises you to cook soufflé potatoes only for your closest friends, because in all likelihood, 'either you will spoil the potatoes or you will spend your evening apologizing for neglecting your guests'. This is Davidism with a human face and a smile of complicity. But the moment I realized that Pomiane was not just sympathetic but deeply on my side came in his recipe for *Bœuf à la Ficelle* (top rump suspended in boiling water by a string). When it is done, you are told to: 'Lift the beef from the saucepan and remove the string. The meat is grey outside and not very appetizing. At this moment you may feel a little depressed.' Isn't that one of the most cheering and pedant-friendly lines a cook ever wrote? 'You may feel a little depressed.' Perhaps, as well as cooking time and number of portions, recipes should also carry a Depression Probability rating. From one to five hangman's nooses.

Pomiane deserves attention (and reprinting) because his is the sort of brasserie and bistro food it is harder and harder to find in France nowadays. After decades of cooking dauphi-

nois potatoes the same way, I was instantly converted to his version; sloppier, creamier, the surface an eruption of umber bubbles, it took me back years and kilometres. Elizabeth David called one of his recipes – for a mountainous version of cheese on toast – 'the best kind of cookery writing', by which she meant that it was 'courageous, courteous, adult'. She goes on: 'It is creative . . . because it invites the reader to use his own critical and inventive faculties, sends him out to make discoveries, form his own opinions, observe things for himself, instead of slavishly accepting what the books tell him.' Well, perhaps, though I think that's pushing the envelope of optimism. All I can say is, the first time I cooked *Bœuf à la Ficelle*, I slavishly accepted everything Edouard de Pomiane told me; and as a result came out of the experience remarkably undepressed.

NO, I WON'T DO THAT

We are in the kitchen of a professional household in London; late 1995 or early 1996. It is dinner time; guests are ambling in and waiting to be seated at a long scrubbed table. On a sideboard is a plate on which squats something circular, brown and sloshy, and definitely not looking its best – a kind of cowpat, really.

SYMPATHETIC GUEST: Chocolate Nemesis?

HOSTESS: Yes.

SYMPATHETIC GUEST: Didn't work?

HOSTESS: No.

SYMPATHETIC GUEST: Never does.

HOSTESS: I've made a couple of other puddings instead.

The key elements in this scene are:

(1) The instinctive and sincere sympathy on the part of the Guest, who has been in the Hostess's position not long previously.

(2) The fact that the pudding, despite not working, is nevertheless displayed openly, as proof that it has been attempted.

(3) The fact that two other puddings have been made to compensate for this extremely high-tariff failure.

Moralists know that Hubris inevitably leads to Nemesis, but never before had the theory been given such literal expression. Overweening pride in one's ability to cook had led to chocolate disaster. The pudding – in case you need reminding – was a signature dish (as the vile phrase has it) of the River Cafe. People had eaten at the restaurant, discovered this most decadent of puddings (1½ lbs chocolate, 10 whole eggs, 1 lb butter, 1 lb 5 oz sugar), and when the first River Cafe Cook Book came out, decided to try it for themselves.

Why it went wrong we Nemetics never discovered. The paranoid explanation was that some key element of the recipe had been deliberately omitted, thereby driving customers back to the restaurant for the authentic item. The more plausible one was that there is a difference between the professional and the domestic oven, that certain dishes exaggerate this difference, and Chocolate Nemesis exaggerated the exaggerations. But the failure was generally so spectacular that few got back up off the floor and tried it again.

This is one of the earliest lessons to be learnt: there are certain dishes always best eaten in restaurants, however tempting the cookbook version appears. In my experience, these frequently turn out to be puddings. That perfect apple tart with parchment-thin but effortlessly crispy base and the shimmering glaze on top? Forget it. Ditto anything dependent on the tatin principle of inversion. Oh, and there is a spectacular yoghurt cake at Moro restaurant in north London which, the only time I tried to make it from their cookbook, tasted wonderful, but looked like something regurgitated. So I tend to read pudding recipes, sigh, and get out the ice-cream machine again.

When the first *River Cafe Cook Book* came out – the blue one – it drew high praise followed by a certain raillery. Some suspected they were having a lifestyle package thrust at them; others felt the emphasis on just this kind of olive oil and just those kinds of lentils was a little discouraging. As James Fenton put it in the *Independent* at the time: 'I've been picking it up and putting it down for weeks now. I can't say I've actually cooked anything from it. More, what I'm doing is deciding whether I can live up to its exacting standards.'

River Cafe Blue led to River Cafe Yellow and Green. I use Blue and Green constantly; though almost always for pasta dishes, risottos, and vegetables. The recipes are clear and largely pedant-proof, the results consistently delicious. And they have taught me more lessons than most. Lesson Two: that the relationship between professional and domestic cook has similarities to a sexual encounter. One party is normally more experienced than the other; and either party should have the right, at any moment, to say, 'No, I'm not going to do that.'

The professional might – like Elizabeth David, for instance – refuse to hand-hold or sweet-talk the punter. While from the punter's point of view, the refusal is more likely to come from (where else?) the gut. For instance, you buy a chicken, take it home, run your hand along the kitchen bookshelf, and decide today is the day for River Cafe Blue. First recipe: Pollo Alla Griglia. Sounds about right: Marinated Grilled Chicken. You read the recipe carefully and discover that the first three-quarters of it are devoted to boning the fowl. And you think: No, I'm not going to do that. Perhaps if they'd called it 'cutting the flesh off the chicken' I might have been up for it. But first, I don't trust my skill. Second, I doubt there's anything in the kitchen drawer which qualifies as a boning knife. And third and conclusively, I've only got one sodding chicken and I don't want to find myself an hour from now faced with something that looks as if a fox has got at it. So that's decided. Turn the page and look at the other River Cafe Blue recipes for chicken. There are two of them. Both start by telling you to bone the damn thing. Well, Hello Delia again.

Lesson Two, Part Two. It's not just difficulty, it's also time. River Cafe Green has a terrific recipe for Penne with Tomato and Nutmeg (and basil, garlic, and pecorino), which I make regularly; the nutmeg is the key surprise element. But I did first have to overcome the recipe's opening sentence: '2.5 kg ripe cherry vine tomatoes, halved and seeded.' So that's well over five pounds of cherry tomatoes. And how many of the little buggers do you think you get to the pound? I'll tell you: I've just weighed fifteen and they came to four ounces. That's sixty to the pound. So we're talking 300, cut in half, 600 halves, juice all over the place, flicking out the seeds 600 times with a knife, worrying about not extracting every single one. All together now: NO, WE'RE

NOT GOING TO DO THAT. Leave the seeds in and call it extra roughage.

These may sound like negative lessons, but they can be as valuable as positive ones. You are discovering – painfully, a little humiliatingly – that you are not up to this because you are not a professional chef and you don't have a larderful of Jamies all panting to deseed tiny tomatoes and being paid to do so. You are by yourself, at home, under pressure of time, and you would very much prefer not to make a hash of dinner.

In any case, what do cookbook writers want? Mute obeisance? What sort of relationship would that imply? You're not a spud-bashing squaddie after all, and they can't put you on a charge for insolence, dumb or otherwise. Remind yourself who paid money for whose book. The only way to earn their respect is to rebel. Go on: it's good for you. It's probably good for them too.

The other evening, I found myself back at that long scrubbed table. The cheese was cleared away, whereupon pudding was laid down in a manner casual almost to the point of cockiness. And yes, it was Chocolate Nemesis, perfectly cooked, utterly delicious, inviting no barnyard comparisons. This time from the new book, *River Cafe Easy*, where it is called Easy Small Nemesis (not a concept those old Greeks would have understood). The ingredients are now halved, but the main difference between the two recipes is in cooking speed: 30 minutes or so at gas mark 3 has become 50 minutes at gas mark ½. Lingering on the stoop, I congratulated the cook on her refusal to accept defeat. Everything had indeed come out for the best in this best of all possible worlds. She chuckled and lowered her voice: 'It still took half as long again as they said.'

THE CACTUS AND
THE SLIPPER

When I was a boy, my parents used to furnish our house from local auction sales. Thus we had an antique television set the size of a child's tree house; its 'wardrobe-style' double doors ate up half a can of polish every time. On top of this vast machine sat a family Bible, also booty from an auction. I once asked why this item was so displayed, given that none of us ever went to church. My mother gave me to understand that it was the sort of thing people in our circumstances tended to have. Inside the front cover was a family tree of the previous owners, who had presumably died out or lost their faith. How strange, I thought, to have the family Bible of another family.

In the kitchen was a family Bible of a different kind, equally an indicator of class, equally acquired second-hand at auction: *Mrs Beeton's Book of Household Management*, in the 1915 Ward Lock edition. It was a real porker of a book, four inches thick and 1,997 pages long. My mother accorded it active respect, covering its boards and art nouveau spine with transparent Fablon. The text held little interest for me at the time, but the multiple plates in both monochrome and full colour fascinated me. There were, for instance, seventeen pages illustrating how to fold napkins: the art of constructing The Boar's Head and The Bishop, The Flat Sachet, The Cactus and The Slipper. Each could only be made from a vast canopy of the purest linen, freshly laundered and lightly starched. There was evidently little point in experimenting with the limp and smeary cotton item that I daily rolled up and stuffed into my Bakelite serviette ring.

And that was just the napkins. The rest of the book had the same combination of weirdness and luxury. Had people ever lived like this? my suburban mind wondered. Somewhere, might they still be doing so? Perhaps there really were houses with a butler's pantry; perhaps voluptuaries really did pile slag heaps of soft fruit on to stemmed porcelain display plates, and serve dishes of stuffed quail in the shape of a Ruritanian crown. Were there really as many soups in the world as the colour plates indicated? And look at this line-up of liquors: twenty-eight bottles crammed into a single picture, Chateau Lafite next to Emu Brand Burgundy. Finally, did – could – anyone have anything resembling 'Illustration 1: The Kitchen'? Component parts: a towering Welsh dresser, huge tables, a station clock, and there, standing unignorably in the corner, hands behind her back, a plump and dutiful cook. How could any of this possibly apply to our life?

It didn't much. Mrs Beeton was occasionally used as an authority of last resort, like the dictionary. 'Let's look it up in Mrs Beeton,' my mother would say, though she was more likely to consult the household and medical notes ('Liniment for Unbroken Chilblains') than the recipes. Having Mrs Beeton on your shelf was like having a chromolithograph of Queen Victoria on the wall, or a toby jug of Florence Nightingale. It was both reassuring and a vaguely patriotic statement. Vicky and Flo-No, however, both lived to a great age, indeed surviving into the twentieth century. Isabella Beeton was born in 1836 and died at the age of only 28, having been delivered of four children and a cookbook. Conan Doyle, in his study of married life, *A Duet, with an Occasional Chorus*, has his heroine say: 'Mrs Beeton must have been the finest housekeeper in the world. Therefore, Mr Beeton must have been the happiest and most comfortable man.' Not, alas, for very long.

The *Book of Household Management* went on growing to monumentality without her; my 1915 edition is about twice the length of the 1861 version. Mrs Beeton became, after her death, a construct, a brand; also, a goddess in the sense of one who defies mortality. As Elizabeth David pointed out, early reprints of her book carried an obituarial note from the widowed Beeton. But Ward Lock, which bought the copyright from the grieving relict, later suppressed this item, allowing readers to imagine – perhaps even as late as 1915 – that some mob-capped matriarch was out there still keeping an eye on them.

When I finally inherited our family kitchen Bible, I found a brochure tucked into it: my grandmother's copy of the Women's Institute 'Introduction to Soft-Slipper Making' – which looks no harder than, say, a Heston Blumenthal recipe. I also re-examined the text. Some of the weirdness remained: a recipe for roast corncrake, another for tinned grouse (open the tin, take out the grouse, roast it). I wondered how, as a child, I had missed the entry under Typical Australian Dishes for Roasted Wallaby (ingredients: '1 Wallaby, veal forcemeat No. 396, milk, butter'); or how, as a prurient adolescent, I had failed to find the wicked passage about what to look out for when examining a potential wet-nurse's breasts.

Food insiders tend to prefer Eliza Acton (1799–1859), many of whose recipes Mrs Beeton transcribed. The editors of the *Dictionary of National Biography* favoured her too: Acton, being a poet as well, made it into the very first volume in 1885; Beeton had to wait for the apologetic 'Missing Persons' volume of 1993. The reputation of *Mrs Beeton*, as opposed to Mrs Beeton, has also taken some stick: Christopher Driver in *The British at Table* (1983) wrote that the book's 'progressive debasement' under successive revisers and enlargers 'may either explain or be explained by the relative stagnation and want of refinement in the indigenous cooking of Britain between 1880 and 1930'.

I'm not sure I'd actually choose to cook from my copy: scallops stewed for sixty minutes or mint sauce made with a quarter of a pint of vinegar to four dessertspoons of mint make the contemporary palate wince. But both Mrs Beeton and *Mrs Beeton* remain classically Victorian in the best sense: encyclopaedic, deeply systematic, rational, progressive, and humane (see the pages on child care). Far from being bull-dog-British, *Household Management* exhibits a proper cultural cringe in the face of French cookery and eating habits. Far from being over-luxurious, it was in its time an attempt to combine good living with economy. Precise cost – down to the nearest penny – is listed alongside cooking times and the number of servings each dish should provide.

Apart from anything else, this reminds us of the stability of money – and the assumption of its future stability. In its certainties and expectations, timetables and costings, Mrs Beeton resembles nothing so much as Baedeker: helping make the kitchens run on time, smoothing your transit to Destination Dinner. So there are lengthy, multiple-choice menu suggestions: for each month of the year, you are offered four different, and differently priced, ways of feeding eight people. If it is April, the top dinner (Clear Leafy Soup via Pigeon and Leg of Lamb to Garibaldi Cream and Farced Olives) will set you back £2/2/6d; the cheapest (Cream of Barley Soup via Stewed Trout and Fillets of Beef to College Pudding and Anchovy Rolls) comes in at £1/9/5d. Note that fivepence: not even rounded up to sixpence. What sublime confidence; except that these costings come from the 1915 edition, published just as the world which the book represents, with all its certainties and optimistic rationalism, its deferential servants and fantastical napkins, was already being blown apart.

THE TOOTH FAIRY

'It doesn't look like the picture,' the Pedant remarked the other day as he laid down the dinner: two plates of Pork Chops with Chicory. His tone did, admittedly, contain a grinding of self-pity.

'That's like believing in the tooth fairy,' replied She For Whom the Pedant Cooks.

It was a fair cop. Why, having arrived, after years of heroic struggle, at a certain modicum of culinary wisdom, do we so lamentably fail to take our own advice? Only a few pages ago, I was coming on all helpful about the deceptions of photography, advising you never to make a dish on the basis of an alluring picture. I may even have uttered harsh words about the stylists and food-fluffers who make things look preternaturally toothsome for the lens.

The text for today is Nigel Slater's *Real Cooking*, pages 106–7. 'Chops and Chicory' occupies a double-page spread, with three photographs across the top: two in black and white showing early stages, one in colour celebrating the lustrous final product. I promise you that I barely glanced at these before deciding to make the dish. I'm not that stupid. Not that early, anyway.

The attractions of the recipe were:

(1) it's a one-pot meal;

(2) like others, I'm on a Ulyssean quest for pork that doesn't end up tasting like the sort of compressed cardboard from which they make hospital pee-bottles;

(3) all you do with the chicory is split it lengthwise in half and bung it in raw with the chops.

There are still a lot of recipes around instructing you to parboil chicory to rid it of its bitterness. This traditional purging inevitably turns the vegetable into a grey sog, and is not only unnecessary but probably counter-productive. Richard Olney says that parboiling actually increases any bitterness present. Elizabeth David credits *le grand* Edouard de Pomiane with first pointing out 'the only way [the non-orthodox way] to braise Belgian endive with success – no water, no blanching, just butter and slow cooking'.

So you are told to take a 'large shallow pan' with a lid, brown the chops on one side in oil and butter, add some fennel seeds, turn the chops over and add, 'face down', the two split 'plump' heads of chicory. Face down, obviously, because you want to get a good caramelly burn to them. My large shallow lidded pan has a diameter of ten inches; it is larger than my two other shallow lidded pans and is – I am speculating here, I admit – probably about the same size as the average largest shallow lidded pan of the average person who cooks from Nigel Slater. Now, you already have in your pan a pair of pork chops, which are – as Mr Slater notes in that friendly way of his which at times of stress can seem mildly irritating – 'as big as your hand'. By dint of brutal jostling, I managed to persuade one single chicory half to lie down between the two chops. Hmm. It was at this moment that my eye caught the middle illustration above the recipe, which shows a pair of hands – presumably the pork-chop sized ones of Mr Slater himself – grinding pepper over his own two immaculately browned chops. There seems to my eye very little room left round the edge of his 'large shallow pan' for all the chicory. Half a plump chicory – to be pedantic about the matter – is seven-and a half inches long, two-and-a-half-inches across at its widest point, and one-and-a-half at its base. Four halves, placed face down, will therefore take up an area of approximately sixty square inches. That's a lot of pan.

So someone was lying. With a cookish oath, I left the bullied half-chicory in place, crammed a couple more edgeways down the side of the chops, and put the fourth (the one I have just measured) back in the fridge. First crisis over. Next you pour in a glass of white wine, turn down the heat, and simmer for fifteen minutes. Another crackle of paranoia went through me at this point. Fifteen minutes? Pomiane braises chicory for forty minutes; Richard Olney for an hour 'or more'. Still, carry on obeying orders. After a quarter of an hour, the chops were done. So: lift them and the chicory out, turn up the heat, add a knob of butter to the pan, stir fast, 'scraping any gooey bits into the melted butter', then 'tip the golden, bitter, buttery juices' over the chops.

Well, no, I didn't do that. For a start, the chicory was still pretty unyielding to a knifepoint, and barely coloured (unlike the ones in the photo). Second, there wasn't the slightest trace of a 'gooey bit' in the pan. And third, my eye caught the final picture, in which a tablespoonful of dark brown concentrated juice was being dripped over a chop.

'They're lying again!' I shouted. (It is a cry often heard from the Pedant's kitchen, and She For Whom knows to treat it as mere aural punctuation.)

Consider: you start with two tablespoons of oil, plus butter; you have added a glass of wine; there is the fat from the chops and the juice from the chicory. What do you get after fifteen minutes on a low heat with the lid on? You get about half a pint of something looking like pale veal stock. You're not told to reduce it; yet Nigel's third picture, on forensic examination, reveals the black splatter of heavy reduction.

I set the chops aside, left the chicory in the pan, and boiled the shit out of it. Thus did this 'thirty-minute supper' become a forty-minute one. From time to time, I would scrape at the squeaky-clean bottom of the pan with a wooden spatula, growling 'Gooey bits, gooey bits' in a tone some might judge filled with wise yet fierce irony and others might find barking mad. Eventually, the dish was delivered to the table, and the following lessons were absorbed.

(1) Most pork still tastes like power-crushed cardboard (not Mr Slater's fault).

(2) The reduced juices in this recipe are utterly delicious; and the fennel seeds actively useful.

(3) This seems to me to be a two-pot dish, both because of the territorial problems and because the chicory ought to cook for longer than the pork. (Though the Pedant isn't entirely convinced by his own argument, given that the juices may only taste so good because of the one-potness. So perhaps you do the chicory by itself for half an hour, then add it with its juices when you start the chops: i.e. a one-and-a-half-pot supper.)

(4) All cookbook photos give us false expectations, even the honest ones. Because here's the irony. When I turned to the introduction of *Real Cooking*, I found Nigel Slater pointing out that the pictures in his book are real too: 'totally natural, not set up or contrived in the typical way of food photographs'. He just cooked away, while the photographer just snapped away. On reflection, this makes it worse, incomparably worse. These pictures haven't been fiddled with, and yet the food they depict still suppurates with glamour compared to anything the average punter turns out.

(5) It is, apparently, a statistical truth that, faced with a book in which some recipes are illustrated and others are not, the hesitating cook will unfailingly prefer the illustrated one. Maybe we imagine the picture confers higher status; maybe we want advance confirmation of what our supper

will look like. Either way, this is foolish. If the mind holds no pre-existing image, then reality has less to fall short of.

(6) Do you remember line drawings? As in Elizabeth David? Evocative without being punitive.

(7) While Mr Slater is clearly on the side of the angels, I think I have spotted a gap in the cookbook market. There are texts that offer us exciting challenges and there are texts designed to reassure us. One lot marked *For Those with Extra Skill, Time and Money*, another labelled *Any Dunce Can Knock This Together*. What about something in between, provisionally entitled *Good Recipes That Prove A Bit Harder Than They Look*? Or, more punchily, *Real Recipes*. Do you think that might catch on?

GOOD THINGS

In China it's taken as a compliment if the tablecloth immediately surrounding your place is, by the end of a meal, a site of major spillage: ill-aimed rice, gouts of soy sauce, twigs from your bird's nest soup or whatever. At least, this is what I was once told by a courteous Chinese guide, who might just have been making the round-eyes feel less embarrassed about their cack-handed chopstick technique.

The same principle applies – without any shadow of ambiguity – to cookbooks. The more decorated their pages are with stove-splash, peel-drip, edible Rorschach stains, oil starbursts, beetroot thumbprints and general incoherent dribblings, the more you have honoured them. By this token – and also by normal rational deduction – my favourite cookery text is Jane Grigson's *Vegetable Book*. To be sure, there are some lively blackcurrant markings in her *Fruit Book*, some lemon blobs and discarded pin-bones in her *Fish Cookery*; but the *Vegetable Book* bears the marks of long-term and heroic kitchen carnage. It also bears that other sign of popularity: the insertion of so many newspaper clippings that the book bulges out wider than its own spine. They are there for the simple reason that whenever Cabbage or Beetroot or Parsnip come to mind, the arm reaches automatically for Grigson, which becomes the obvious repository for other people's recipes on the same subject.

Unless a cookbook is nothing more than a collection of plagiarisms, a sense of its author's personality will inevitably come through. Sometimes this is a mistake – that personality may be authoritarian, snobbish, effete, dull. The author, for all their technical expertise in understanding ingredients, may not have a clue about what is going on inside the human beings who buy and use their book. Anthony Lane, reviewing the scarily efficient Martha Stewart, quotes this typical piece of advice about having folks round for a bite: 'One of the most important moments on which to expend extra effort is the beginning of a party, often an awkward time, when guests feel tentative and insecure.' To which Lane exactly responds: 'The guests are insecure? How about the frigging cook?'

There is no such cult of personality in Grigson: rather, her presence suffuses her writing like some familiar and warming herb in a stew. You are constantly aware of it, the stew couldn't have been made without it, yet you don't keep having to pick it out from between your teeth. Her authorial mode is that of a very well-informed friend who has confidence in your ability at the stove. She is historical, anecdotal, personal where it is relevant – recalling, for instance, her grandmother's belief that peeled cucumbers were great provokers of wind – but mainly she subsumes herself into her subject. She is scholarly without being dry, generous without being subservient.

Some cookery writers will brazenly present a book of recipes as if they had all been invented from scratch in the immediate months before publication; Grigson both cites and celebrates original sources and other people's recipes. Some cookery writers are smugly contemporary, exuding a sense of superiority to the old days, when they knew less and had fewer ingredients; Grigson regards the present not as the culminating point on an ever-rising curve of technology and nous, but as one moment in an ancient and continuing process. Indeed, we are in many ways less sophisticated and less successful cooks than previous generations. Machinery has made us lazy; the acceleration of life has made us impatient; air-freight and the deep-freeze have thinned our sense of the seasons; while the easy availability of foreign produce makes us disdain our own. Seakale was a particular point of reference for Grigson: why do we chase after *cavolo nero* when seakale – grown by Thomas Jefferson, compared by Carême to celery and asparagus – is forgotten?

Grigson's scholarship was considerable but unostentatious. Here she is on cabbage: 'It is easy to grow, a useful source of greenery for much of the year. Yet as a vegetable it has original sin and needs improvement. It can smell foul in the pot, linger through the house with pertinacity, and ruin a meal with its wet flab. Cabbage also has a nasty history of being good for you. Read Pliny, if you do not believe me.' We do, of course, believe her, but her mode of expression also convinces us that it might be fun to look up Pliny. Further on in her introduction to cabbage lies a story about Descartes. A 'lively Marquise', who shared the common presumption of the time that high thinking should be matched by austere living, once came across the philosopher tucking into more than was strictly necessary to keep a hermit alive. When she expressed her surprise, Descartes responded, 'Do you think that God made good things only for fools?' This story, which Grigson clearly found emblematic, gave her the title for her collection *Good Things*.

Her reassurance that the past is constantly alive encouraged me to cook dishes that otherwise I wouldn't have attempted, like Toulouse-Lautrec's Gratin of Pumpkin. This didn't quite pan out, though at least it confirmed that Lautrec had a great sense of colour. On the other hand, Montaigne's Potatoes Cooked with Pears, a dish the essayist discovered on his way through Switzerland to Italy in 1580 (and which goes sweetly with ham), aptly confirms that while our eating habits have changed, the structure of our palates hasn't.

Jane Grigson was married to Geoffrey Grigson, who for decades was the most caustic and dismissive literary critic in the country; so – on the page, anyway – they represented a Jack and Mrs Sprat of temperaments. Not that Jane Grigson was a food luvvie – her views were always very clear, never soggy. She knew what she didn't like and what didn't work. Wild cabbage is 'very nasty indeed'; most English turnips are only 'suitable for the over-wintering of herds, schoolchildren, prisoners, and lodgers'. She is also very sound on swede.

At times, though, her natural benignity verged on utopianism. Here she imagines the British nation enthusiastically going back to vegetable growing, wherever they might live. 'Now we might extend the picture to include high-rise blocks, patched with vegetation on every balcony – Marmande and plum tomatoes in pots, herbs in window-boxes, courgettes and squashes trailing round the doors. Inside, there could be aubergine, pepper, chilli, and basil plants on the window sill, jars of sprouting seeds, dishes of mustard and cress, with mushroom buckets and blanching chicory in the dark broom and airing cupboards.'

It has to be said that, twenty-five years on from these words, the main problems of inner-city estates do not come from noxious whiffs of thyme and basil or from old ladies tripping over trailing courgettes on walkways. But perhaps cookery writers tend by nature to be optimists. (Imagine a cookbook written by a confirmed grouch: 'Well, I shouldn't think this will work, and it'll probably taste vile, but you might, if you can be bothered. . .') Jane Grigson was not just a Good Thing herself, she was exemplary. Her *Vegetable Book* is prefaced by a quote from Robert Louis Stevenson: 'Every book is, in an intimate sense, a circular letter to the friends of him who writes it.' Yes: but the best books persuade readers who do not even know the author that they are friends of hers as well.

SERVICE WITH
A SCOWL

Marcella Hazan, in her omnium gatherum *The Essentials of Classic Italian Cooking*, has a recipe for Baked Bluefish Fillets with Potatoes, Garlic and Olive Oil, Genoese Style. I went to a fishmonger's I tend to enter with a certain trepidation. They sell good produce, they accept your money; but you often have to endure a laugh-in from a pair of tattooed comedians.

'Have you got any bluefish?' I asked.

'Bluefish,' the monger repeated as if it were no more than a feed line. 'We've got white fish, pink fish, yellow fish...' As he scanned his slab for further hues of jocularity, my heart sank.

Cooking begins with shopping, and while I doubt I shall ever take a cookery course, I might willingly sign up for a shopping course. Resident experts would have to include a nutritionist, a food writer, a games-theorist and a psychologist. I remember being taken shopping by my mother in the aftermath of rationing and first becoming aware of the freighted nature of this everyday process. She was the monetary and social boss, he (and that's one of the problems – it always was and usually remains a he) had control of supply; she knew what she wanted, he knew what he had; she might decline to pay a certain price, he might decline to offer what she needed, even though he had it. The whole exchange felt pointlessly about power – and still does sometimes – with an occasional snifter of class warfare. At best, a certain complicity was possible, but rarely more than a factitious equality.

This is why the Pedant's morale is rarely lifted by a recipe beginning 'Instruct your butcher to. . .' or 'Telephone your fishmonger in advance and ask. . .' Now I know some excellent butchers, fishmongers, and fruit 'n' veggers, though I don't think of any of them as 'mine'. Equally, I sometimes encounter a needlessly surly butcher who, when you hesitantly propose what you might require, will seize something in a flurry of hands, offer it for a nanosecond's inspection with a lip-curling 'That do?', and have it on the scales and off again before your eyes can refocus, while calling out a price which for all you know could well be a touch speculative.

Yet he sells excellent meat. The only time Mr Needlessly Surly softened his act was during the BSE crisis, though the sight of innate surliness overlaid with temporary ingratiation wasn't for the squeamish. The unlovely success of supermarkets is due to many factors, but eliminating a potentially awkward social exchange is by no means a minimal one. If you study those serving in the butchery departments of supermarkets, they may be dressed like butchers, but they lack the character; they have the polite, unthreatening manner of corporate employees trained to euphemize the fact that meat comes from dead animals.

The answer, of course, is more knowledge, and thus confidence, on the customer's part. Cookbooks usually begin with descriptions of equipment and culinary processes; but shopping nous is taken for granted. Most of us go out equipped with a pathetic rag-bag of hand-me-down knowledge. Fish: inspect the eye to gauge freshness. Oysters: only when there's an R in the month. Pineapples: test for ripeness by pulling at a leaf – inner or outer, I can never remember which – to see if it comes away easily in the hand (try that in some shops). Meat: ask your butcher if his meat is well hung (no, you'll have to rephrase that). Small knowledge that betrays wider ignorance, handing the tradesman any advantage he seeks. And then there's another inbuilt problem: you go out with a list of items demanded by an autocratic recipe-writer and something proves unobtainable. Panic and fear of failure begin here.

So all help from cookbooks is gratefully received. For instance, the suggestion of alternative ingredients ('This dish works equally well with white fish, pink fish, yellow fish...'). The writer I find most reassuring in this regard is Marcella Hazan. This came as a surprise when I first started cooking from her. I had always imagined that since Italian cuisine, of all the major European styles, depends on pure and often speedy handling of the freshest ingredients, there was little room for manoeuvre. Hazan freely lists plausible alternatives; is indulgent about dried herbs; actively recommends tinned tomatoes as tasting better than most fresh; often prefers dried porcini to their fresh equivalent. She spares you suffering by noting which dishes can be cooked to which stage ahead of time. She has even – responsive to our indolence and love of convenience – tried 'again and again' to square use of the microwave with the principles of Italian cuisine. Happily, all her attempts have proved utter failures.

But it was with pasta that she produced her greatest

liberating effect on my kitchen. I used to own an electric pasta machine of which I was grossly proud. It would heave and churn and chunter away before extruding through a choice of nozzles whichever pasta you commanded. This had to be immediately and pedantically laid out on kitchen paper to prevent it sticking together; and the machine had to be dismantled and cleaned three seconds after use if the residue of pasta wasn't to set like concrete. But there was an almost excessive satisfaction about the swift transfer to salted, boiling water, to which I always remembered to add a big glug of olive oil, having read somewhere that this helped keep the strands separate. *Pasta della casa?* Yes, anxious work, of course, but it's always better than the bought stuff.

Then I read Marcella Hazan. For a start there was this: 'Never put oil in the water except when cooking stuffed homemade pasta' (to stop the casing from coming apart). And then the incendiary moment: 'There is not the slightest justification for the currently fashionable notion that 'fresh' pasta is preferable to factory-made dry pasta. One is not better than the other, they are simply different . . . They are seldom interchangeable, but in terms of absolute quality, they are fully equal.' And guess what? For years I'd been proudly making the sort of dishes for which dry pasta would have been preferable.

The pasta machine went into the Drawer of Spurned Machinery and Marcella Hazan was beatified. Her recipes not only permit as much latitude as possible, they also produce, in my experience, a higher percentage of successes, and a truer authenticity of taste, than any I know. She gives confidence – enough confidence, perhaps, to make me ring up the tattooed fishmonger one morning and snarl, 'Now listen here: I want to order some bluefish, and don't give me any of your lip!'

ONCE IS ENOUGH

I was ordering some venison by phone from an organic meat farm. Not having dealt with them before, I asked what else they stocked. The female voice ran down a list and ended with 'squirrel'. That sparked a certain interest. Ever since the year the little buggers ate all the buds off a camellia in the garden, I've been looking for some practical means of revenge. The item of vermin seemed remarkably cheap (so it should be) and I was advised that long, slow cooking was preferable. Then I was asked if I wanted the beast jointed.

'What's the advantage?' I asked.

'Well,' came the reply, 'if you don't have it jointed, it does look very like a squirrel.'

I ordered it jointed.

A couple of days later the styrofoam box arrived and I

scrabbled around beneath the venison for the bushy-tailed *amuse-gueule*. I opened the plastic pack. Uh-uh. They'd forgotten to joint it and it looked. . . yes, just like a naked, dead, defurred squirrel. I tried talking tough to it – 'You're just a rat with PR', that sort of thing – but this didn't make it any the more immediately cookable. Eventually I gave it away to a poor student with a woodsman's bent. And I've never been back to order another one.

There are certain things you just can't bring yourself to eat, or cook; or, if done once, do again. I have an omnivorous female friend who refuses to eat only two things: cooked oysters and sea urchin. When asked what she had against sea urchin, she replied, 'It tastes of warm snot.' This description somehow had a prophylactic effect on me for a number of years, although I did eventually succumb to a sea-urchin soufflé in a Paris restaurant when someone else was paying (through the nose). It tasted. . . no, no, it was really quite. . . look, I can't exactly find the words for it.

I once bought an eel from a Chinese fishmonger in Soho, carried it home on the Northern Line, and then realized my next job was to skin it. This is what you have to do: nail it to a door-frame or other substantial wooden part of your dwelling, make an incision on either side of the neck, take a pair of pliers in each hand, grip the two cut pieces of skin, put your foot against the door level with the eel's head, and slowly haul back the skin, which is firm and elasticated, like a dense inner tube. Afterwards I was glad to have done it. Now I shall know how to proceed if forced to survive somewhere with only an eel, two pairs of pliers, and a door-frame for company; but I don't otherwise need the activity to be central to my life. Smoked, stewed, barbecued – eel is welcome on my plate in most forms; but from now on I'll let others do the skinning.

I've eaten snake once, crocodile once, water buffalo once. Ditto those 100-year-old eggs the Chinese bury in the ground and then (like squirrels) dig up after a season or so, and which to my palate taste like old hard-boiled eggs that have been buried in the ground for a long time. I ate kanga-roo at a literary dinner in Australia with Kazuo Ishiguro, who ordered it with the words, 'I always like to eat the national emblem.' ('What does he eat in England?' a nearby poet growled at me, 'Lion?') I intend to eat rook now the walking season is under way: there's a pub in the Chilterns that does it to special order. I've even eaten a Big Mac just the once, but let's not lower the tone of the column.

None of this much impresses my friend the travel-writer

Redmond O'Hanlon, for whom croc is as routine as a kipper. His alimentary canal has down the years played host to cayman, capybara, rat, agouti, armadillo, monkey, monitor lizard, maggots, palm-grubs, and other life forms. But this in its turn fails to impress O'Hanlon's teenage son, Galen. The last time his father musingly ran through his list of gastronomic exotica, Galen interrupted with, 'Yes, but you've got no taste buds, Dad, so it's of no interest what you've eaten.'

Generally, you eat things once and never again from lack of opportunity rather than distaste (the crocodile was strangely various, as I remember – there were three different cuts served on the same plate, one of them tending towards meat, another towards fish and the third poised in between). No doubt in the future some of our eating habits will be high-mindedly condemned as shameful and disgusting and incomprehensible. Rather as we feel when we learn that they used to eat herons in the late Middle Ages and Renaissance; further, that they trained falcons to hunt them. The English roasted heron with ginger, the Italians with garlic and onions; the Germans and Dutch made them into pies; the French thought it bad form to serve heron without any sauce, and La Varenne further suggested decorating the plat-

ter with flowers to make the dish look more appealing. These curiosa come from *The Wilder Shores of Gastronomy*, a pungent anthology derived from Alan Davidson's magazine *Petits Propos Culinaires*.

But there are also dishes you cook once, and which, in their way, have gone reasonably well – several small routine disasters in the preparation, but nothing out of the ordinary, nothing to prevent you seeing what, in a perfect world, they might taste like. Nonetheless, for external reasons, you are unable to contemplate ever making them again. Perhaps one of your guests threw up in the street outside – anyway, some minor psychological impediment rises up whenever, a year or two down the line, the cookbook falls open again at that page.

I once made Hare in Chocolate Sauce for a retired admiral. Does that sound like a good menu selection to you or not? It was certainly a questionable call in that I'd never tried the dish out on anyone else before. The Admiral was in his seventies, a fierce and personable man with a certain amorous back-story. From the supper table he looked around him and noted that there were pictures on the wall.

'My father used to do a bit of this. . . art stuff,' he remarked.

I knew — and he knew that I knew, and I knew that he knew that I knew — that his father had been about the most famous British painter of his day. Some sort of marker was being put down. When it became clear that the Pedant was in charge of the galley that evening, and, moreover, was proposing a main course that sounded like plain cooking mucked around with, I felt myself the object of a less than entirely dispassionate gaze.

The recipe came from Jane Grigson's *Good Things*. When the stew is cooked, you start preparing the sauce by melting sugar in a saucepan until it turns pale brown, and then adding some wine vinegar. It is meant to fuse into a rich syrup, to which chocolate, pine kernels, candied peel, and so on are added. Instead, with violent insubordination, it let off a broadside of flash and fizzle and turned on the spot into some sort of sour caramel crunch. There was no bluffing my way out of this one. The hare was waiting on one side, the final ingredients on another; they could only meet with the help of this facilitating sauce.

I got out a new pan and was apprehensively melting the sugar when I heard the Admiral declaring his passion for She For Whom the Pedant Cooks. This was somewhat unexpected to me, and to her, and, by the sound of it, to the Admiral himself. His voice was loud and exact, as befits someone used to giving orders.

'What does one do when one falls in love?' he was asking in a non-rhetorical way, words that have somehow stuck with me ever since.

The sugar began to melt just as my heart, I have to confess, was hardening a little. My nose was in the cookbook, but my ears were aimed towards the dining room, so maybe my concentration wasn't at its fullest. I arrived again at the key moment of gastro-fusion, and exactly the same violent explosion took place all over again. Was this some sort of goddamned metaphor? Well, I'm sorry, Admiral, but the menu has changed. We're having Hare with Chocolate but without Proper Sauce. The sauce is in the bilges. Oh, and do be sure to watch out for any dangerous bones that might lodge in the throat.

And since that night I've never once been tempted to make Hare in Chocolate Sauce again. Though I have from time to time found myself wondering what roast admiral might taste like. Squirrel, I suspect.

NOW THEY TELL ME!

Not long after the Case of the Amorous Admiral and the Exploding Saucepan, I found myself in correspondence with Jane Grigson about Flaubert's diet. (He was more a trencherman than a gourmet; he once ate dromedary in Egypt; his favourite delicacies were mandarins and oysters.) I took the chance to mention, in as neutral terms as possible, the hazards of adding wine vinegar to molten sugar in a hot saucepan.

'This is always a bit tricky,' she replied consolingly, and went on to suggest how to minimize the Krakatoa effect. (You take the pan off the heat first: yeah, yeah, obvious, I know, should have thought of that. . .) Then she told me how it could be avoided completely: 'In fact nowadays I put the two ingredients into the pan together

– this is nouvelle-cuisine style – and boil them to a caramel together.'

Now she tells me! I reflected ruefully.

Some time later, a chef friend explained in his weekly column a New Easy Method of making risotto. As any domestic cook who's ever made one knows, it's virtually impossible to do anything during the final twenty minutes or so except stir, add liquid, worry; stir, add liquid, worry, and so on. At best you might have time to leave the hob just long enough to shake an ice-cube into a de-stressing drink; normal sociability is quite out of the question.

But apparently a solution was at hand. The new system consisted of doing all the preliminary bits as usual – the onion-sweating, the coating of the rice with the oil or butter, the glass of wine or vermouth – but instead of adding merely the first ladleful of simmering stock and beginning the cycle of worry, you pour in the whole lot at the same time. Then you bring it back to the boil, take it off the heat, shove a lid on, and leave it for the same cooking time as under the old scrape-and-scratch routine. The anxiety is thus substantially reduced: not to zero, of course (it never is), and the fact that you aren't allowed to lift the lid and examine how the thing is getting along does allow negative speculation to enter the mind of the culinary self-doubter. However, more importantly, you have time to prepare a salad, make a whole trayful of drinks, and generally impersonate a normal human being.

I tried the New Easy Method a few times, and there was certainly nothing wrong with it that I can remember. But somehow I drifted back to the traditional technique: maybe I associated the dish too indelibly with unremitting effort at the hob-face, and missed the anxiety. A while later, we went to supper with our friend and found him preparing a risotto – stirring away at the old-fashioned, unlidded version (while also, I admit, preparing about three other things at the same time).

'So what about that system where you just pour in all the stock and leave the lid on?'

'Oh', he replied, 'I don't do it like *that* any more,' as if surprised that anyone did.

Now he tells me! Where had been the recantation in his column? He's changed his mind! That's not meant to happen! But of course it does; and this is one of the harder lessons for the domestic cook to learn. We implicitly assume that those whose instructions we follow have perfected the recipe before printing it. Tried it out with testers, adjusted both the seasoning and the wording until terminal precision is attained, and then handed it over to us. Further, we assume that when they cook their own recipes, they follow each verse of the scripture just as we do. But they don't. You never step into the same stream twice, and a cook never steps into the same recipe twice. The cook, the ingredients, the recipe, and the resulting dish are never exactly the same. It's not exactly post-modernism, and it might be heavy-handed to invoke Heisenberg's Uncertainty Principle, but you know what I mean.

The other evening, Swiss friends who had recently married came to supper and something typically, even strangely, English seemed appropriate. Jane Grigson's Salmon in Pastry with a Herb Sauce (which she attributes to the Hole in the Wall restaurant in Bath) was decided upon. Two thick salmon fillets are made into a sandwich with a filling of butter, currants, and chopped ginger (this insertion of sweetness into fish shows the recipe's medieval origins), then wrapped in pastry and baked for half an hour. The Pedant was in charge of filleting and skinning the salmon; She For Whom He Cooks was responsible for the filling and the herby sauce. Luckily, the recipe occurs in both Grigson's *Fish Cookery*

(1973) and her English Food (1974), so a copy of each lay open, and there was none of the shoulder-barging inherent in shared kitchen use.

She For Whom had mixed the butter and ginger together and called for a tablespoon of currants. I held the bag poised over the spoon.

'Does it say rounded or heaped?' I asked, in a not entirely self-satirical way.

'Neither, so it's neither.'

A pity: I like currants. Still, I obediently chucked in the level tablespoonful and work proceeded. The sauce was now under way on the other side of the kitchen.

'This is a bit vague,' came the word. '*Parsley, chervil, tarragon, chopped. Doesn't say how much.*'

'Typical bloody recipe,' I sympathized, and urged the application of Pedant's Rule 15b. This lays down that when quantities of an ingredient are left unspecified, you should add a lot of any item you like, a little of what you're less keen on, and none at all of what you don't fancy.

The salmon sandwich was constructed, the sauce bubbling, the pastry about to fall under the rolling pin when I asked 'What about the almonds?'

'What almonds?'

'One rounded tablespoon chopped, blanched almonds,' I read from *English Food*.

'That's news to me,' she replied, rescanning *Fish Cookery*.

'Hang on,' I said, 'it is a heaped tablespoon of currants after all. Except it's raisins.'

We compared recipes in our separate books, and these were the differences: almonds in one, not in the other; an unheaped tablespoon of currants versus a heaped tablespoon of raisins; two knobs of ginger versus four knobs; four ounces of butter as against three ounces; unspecified parsley, chervil, and tarragon as against one heaped teaspoon of chopped parsley and one (presumably unheaped) teaspoon of chopped chervil and tarragon mixed.

Well, I prised apart the salmon fillets and we threw in some chopped almonds; also, at my pedantic insistence, a quantity of currants equal to the difference between an unheaped and a heaped tablespoon. I also threw in a mild rant along the following lines: theoretically I know that all recipes are approximations, that the creative cook will each time make adjustments according to the quality and availability of ingredients, that nothing is set in stone (except wine vinegar mixed with hot molten sugar), and so on and so on. I just don't want to be confronted with the reality of this in mid-cook. Oh yes, and another thing: if I'd known that raisins were an alternative, I wouldn't have found myself using currants that were, according to the label, six months past their sell-by date.

To the point, Pedant. How did it taste? Bloody marvellous, actually, though I say it myself – and do so only because I was responsible for the less crucial parts of the preparation. So it didn't matter in the end? No, not really. Then why all this fuss? Because, well, that's what cooking's about, isn't it? It's practically a dictionary definition. Cooking is the transformation of uncertainty (the recipe) into certainty (the dish) via fuss.

And since I won't hear a word against Jane Grigson, even from myself, I began devising explanations. It was a test of some sort, perhaps even a joke; anyway, a deliberate, Grigsonian manoeuvre to teach close and faithful readers a small lesson about Heisenberg's Uncertainty Principle. It was, of course, nothing of the sort, and my few weeks of grousing were terminated when someone pointed out that if I'd carried on reading English Food after the point at which the recipe itself ends, I would have come across the simple words: 'This is a slightly adapted version of. . .' Tom Jaine, whose step-father George Perry-Smith first introduced the dish at the Hole in the Wall, kindly sent me its first printed version from Thomas Dawson's *Good Huswife's Jewell* (c. 1585): 'How to bake a joll [i.e. jowl, the head and shoulders] of fresh salmon: Take ginger and salt, and season it, and certaine currans, and cast them about and under it, and let the paste be fine, and take a little butter and lay it about the paste, and set it in the oven two houres, and serve it.'

Well, at least I didn't have to cook in 1585. There I was moaning about vagueness and variations. Season the salt? Certaine currans? How many currans make certaine? And not a damn gas mark in sight. What would Ye Pedante have done?

KEEP IT SIMPLE

'Help!' began the e-mail. 'What's a twenty-gram egg-yolk? How do I weigh it? If it's too heavy, do I cut it in half?'

Can you guess which cookery writer set off this wail in my inbox? That's right, it's Mr Heston Blumenthal. Do you read his recipes every week? Do you, at least, read their titles? Crushed Meringue and Pistachio with Soya Sauce Mayonnaise? Does that make you feel bracingly challenged or hideously inadequate? Do your salivary glands throb and your feet make pawing gestures in the direction of the kitchen, or do you find yourself musing on the attractive blue neon signs of Pizza Express?

Don't get me wrong. I am in awe of Mr Blumenthal. I once had dinner at his restaurant, The Fat Duck, at Bray and, by ordering very conservatively, had a wonderfully exotic meal. He is a disciple of El Bulli, the staggeringly innovative restaurant north of Barcelona, and this is a brave thing to be in the Home Counties. He is also one of the few restaurateurs in his class and price range who lets you bring your own wine in exchange for a corkage fee. He is that rare mixture of a supreme gastrotechnologist who understands the twitch and flex of every muscle, and a cook who is rococo in his imaginings. If you gave him a human brain he might poach it lightly in a reduction of 1978 Cornas and top it with a mortarboard made of liquorice; but he might not understand all that had been going on inside it before he popped it into the pot.

Again, don't get me wrong. I quite want to cook some of what Mr Blumenthal proposes: though when he tells me that the best way of cooking a steak is to flip it every fifteen seconds, making thirty-two flips in all for its eight-minute cooking period, I am inclined to wonder who will be minding the chips and mushy peas while I flip four steaks 128 times, so I say Pass. As for the chips – did you see his recipe for chips? He takes the 'pause' technique – whereby you lift out the frying basket and let the oil regain its initial temperature before the final browning plunge – to its logical conclusion (or fantastical extreme). The Blumenthal method is to par-fry the chips and then shove them in the fridge to chill out. After a couple of hours or so, you heat up the oil all over again and complete the cooking. I have given this much thought, and cannot imagine anyone – *anyone* – ever doing it.

However, his emphasis on slow cooking seems to me salutary and admirable. And by slow he means very slow. I was cooking oxtail stew the other day and in the usual way found myself checking half a dozen recipes for how long to give it. Alastair Little: two hours (you're joking); Fay Maschler: three; Frances Bissell: four (getting warmer). I think I gave it five, and two subsequent re-heatings of forty-five minutes each only enhanced the tail's fork-meltingness. Mr Blumenthal probably has a recipe that involves giving it the full cycle of the moon.

The sticking-point, however, came fairly early. I had read several of his recipes for slow cooking, in which he gave oven temperatures in centigrade. I have a standard oven with gas marks, and we were clearly talking gas mark 1 and below; the temperature-conversion charts that preface basic cookbooks didn't even start at the temperature (65°) that Mr B. was proposing for one particular recipe. In any case, he said an oven thermometer was absolutely essential; you also had to make sure the heat had stabilized before putting the meat in. Guessing was simply not an option.

Then I remembered that I did actually own an oven thermometer, bought on one of those scavenging trips to a kitchen shop where you go in search of a brave new machine and come back with a paring knife and a questionable gadget. It was, inevitably, in that drawer where you stow such things and then forget about them, where everything is tangled up – whisks with chopsticks through their wires – a shameful place. I dug it out; 65°, I said to myself dreamily. Six hours, seven hours, a day-and-a-half, with cooking odours wafting gently up to my study. I took the thermometer out of its packaging. And its lowest marking was 75°.

Mr Blumenthal is off my radar as well as off my oven thermometer, and that's all there is to be said. His cuisine is Olympian, fit for gods who have become sated and fractious after millennia of ordinary perfection. The more immediate problem of conscience comes with writers who are similarly high-minded, but more accessible. I revere Elizabeth David, yet don't cook from her as often as I know I should or even as often as I want to. Why not? Because she seems to have her admonishing eye on me; because I feel that if I get something wrong I will have offended her shade. Lo, I have been sloppy, and the temple of cookery has been profaned.

Or take the case of the American food writer Richard Olney (1927–99). Like Mrs David, he was a powerful force for good, a fine and evocative describer who put food in a wider cultural context. The Times obituarist rightly said of Olney's Simple French Food that it was 'one of the very few cookbooks everyone should have'. He was also a man of incorrigibly high standards. Years ago I was a restaurant critic and invited to a grand celebration of French cuisine at the Dorchester Hotel. A banquet for 200 or so, prepared by a bucketload of starry Michelin chefs. General bonhomie and savoir vivre. Olney was one of the guests, and I later heard that when the waiter poured him a glass of red wine, he sipped it and sent it back. Not because it was corked, but because it was a couple of degrees too warm.

Simple French Food. Be careful: the first of those three words is booby-trapped. Towards the end of a six-page rumination on the term, Olney comes to the conclusion that 'simplicity is a complicated thing'. The modern mantra goes, 'If food is not simple, it is not good.' Olney prefers its inversion: 'If food is not good, it is not simple.' Thus everything from peasant cooking to classic haute cuisine may, by this definition, be accounted simple. We are not talking about ease of preparation. What we are after is 'purity of effect' – which (you will have guessed by now) may involve considerable complication of means.

The publisher of Simple French Food meanly had the book glued rather than sewn, and the pages you use regularly fall out when you open it. What falls out in my case are Gratinéed Cauliflower Loaf, Courgettes Gratin, Pommes Paillasson (the recipe is alone worth the price of the book) and Marinated Leg of Lamb. Clearly, I have stuck to the simplest of the simple.

The reason is easy to explain. Like most people, I annotate my cookbooks ticks, crosses, exclamation marks, emendations, and suggestions for next time. In certain cases, next time is never. My annotation of Olney's Courgette Pudding Soufflé (and I apologize in advance for the language) goes as follows: This dinner for two took me four hours. The mouli doesn't work as he says, and on turning out the soufflé collapses flat and the sauce became a quarter deep layer on top of it, i.e. a fucking disaster. But all the same fucking delicious! One of many possible mistakes on my part was that I did not own a savarin mould. Own? I didn't even know what one was. Overleaf, where

Olney mentions this item, I see I have underlined his words and written: *Why not explain what this is somewhere in the bloody book, matey?*

As you can see, I emerged from Courgette Pudding Soufflé in a somewhat conflicted state of mind. And no, I didn't go out and buy a savarin mould. I just went back to Gratinéed Cauliflower Loaf. It's partly about admitting the limits of one's ambition; but it's more about one's attitude to failure. And here most people, and certainly most kitchen pedants, part company with Messrs Blumenthal and Olney, and also with Mrs David. It's not that these experts don't think failures occur – they are aware of them. Elizabeth David writes: 'In cooking, the possibility of muffing a dish is always with us. Nobody can eliminate that.' But she would agree with Richard Olney when he writes: 'A failure is no disgrace and may very often be more instructive than a success.'

Yes, I can see that in utopian theory. But in practice, most domestic cooks feel that failure is indeed a disgrace, and it would take some years of therapy to convince them otherwise. So we have over the years developed a very good system for cutting down the likelihood of failure. If we make a dish once and it turns out anything from a serious muff to a complete hash, then we don't cook it again. Ever. It's natural selection in the kitchen. And as a system it is – in the very ordinary sense of the term – simple.

IN THE PURPLE

False etymologies are often more instructive than true ones. Everyone knows, for instance, that the word 'posh' is acronymically derived from 'Port Out, Starboard Home', indicating the more desirable, less sunned upon side of the boat on the long imperial voyage to and from India. What everyone knows, however, is sociologically picturesque, but etymologically without foundation. (The *Oxford English Dictionary* refers doubters to George Chowdharay-Best in *Mariner's Mirror* (1971) Jan. 91–92.)

Similarly, 'mangel-wurzel'. This began life as 'mangold-wurzel', literally 'root of the beet'; but people (German people, that is) misheard it as 'mangel-wurzel', 'root of scarcity'. This was logical since you would only consider eating a wurzel if the ground was frozen and your belly was rumbling. This aural transformation and spelling duly made their way into English. The French, more typically bent on defending their language, translated it literally, giving us *racine de disette*, which preserves the false etymology in aspic.

'Root of scarcity': the French have always had an unbalanced, indeed snooty relationship with root vegetables. They find exaggerated virtue in the turnip; on the other hand, I have yet to meet anyone in France who has knowingly consumed a parsnip. A Frenchwoman recently told me that she herself had never eaten a Jerusalem artichoke, let alone a swede, but she had heard of wretched people being reduced to gnawing on them during the war. This is confirmed by Richard Olney's *Simple French Food*, which has a couple of recipes for turnip, but none at all for parsnip, Jerusalem artichoke, swede – or, for that matter, beetroot. Elizabeth David, in *French Provincial Cooking*, notes fleetingly that parsnip is 'used in very small quantities as a flavouring vegetable for the *pot-au-feu* or for soups.'

Maybe it's something to do with the words themselves. 'Swede' sounds more edible – sort of half-mashed already – in English; whereas '*le rutabaga*' is a chewily indigestible mouthful of phonemes. Ditto '*le topinambour*', whose outsides happen to contain the word '*tambour*' ('drum'), thus seeming

to hint at the timpani-bursts of colonic venting that a really forceful Jerusalem artichoke gives rise to. The 'Jerusalem' part – while we're on the subject of misleading etymologies – doesn't refer to any supposed place of origin, but is a mishearing of the French '*girasol*', 'sunflower', which is generically related to the fartichoke.

I remember being puzzled, when I first went to France, by a road sign frequently glimpsed in rural areas: a red warning triangle bearing the single word BETTERAVES. Why did French farmers harvest and transport this admirable crop so carelessly that they allowed it to become a traffic hazard? In fact, the signs almost certainly referred to sugar beet; even so, to equate *betteraves* with those other non-edible road-threats such as *gravillons*, *chutes de pierres* and *chaussée déformée* seemed a little contemptuous.

But then the beetroot has had a remarkably up-and-down career. Edouard de Pomiane notes that Oribasius, court physician to Julian the Apostate, spoke very ill of it. I casually mentioned this abstruse piece of information in an e-mail to the Aristotelian scholar Jonathan Barnes, only to be told in reply that 'most of Oribasius consists of excerpts copied out of Galen.' Oh, very well then: Galen spoke very ill of the beetroot. He thought it needed boiling twice to be any good, and his praise scarcely registers on the dial: 'I should be surprised if, once boiled, it were any less nutritious than any other plant of the same kind.' Also: 'As a laxative, one would say that it is neither effective nor harmful.'

When first introduced into Britain, in the seventeenth century, it was viewed as a sweet pleasure of various application; there is even an eighteenth-century recipe for 'crimson biscuits of red beet-root'. But native puritanism kicked in at some subsequent point: this is a vegetable which naturally tastes nice and sweet, so let's make it taste nasty and sour. Mrs Beeton offers only two ways of treating it – pickling and boiling; though she does also cite Dr Lyon Playfair's unexciting recipe for cheapo brown bread made by rasping down the root and mixing it with an equal amount of flour. And if this wasn't enough to put you off the vegetable, there were even more recherché methods. A correspondent in Oldham told me that his paternal grandfather refused to touch beet-root because in his youth he had seen it used as a bedding plant in cemeteries. All his life the funereal connotations simply overrode his taste buds.

For the bulk of the past century, generations of schoolchildren learned to wince at rancid roundels staining the delightful spam on their plates. In my own case I associate the root with my grandmother's pickle fork, one of those two-pronged EPNS numbers with a sliding cross-piece to dislodge the stabbed item. Everything which this instrument picked up seemed to my infant mind vilely unpalatable. Indeed, you could deduce as much from the nature of the invention: the dislodging gadget had to be employed because nobody in their right mind would want to touch the disgustingly pickled onion, gherkin, beetroot or whatever with their fingers.

In those days crisps were made only from potatoes; nowadays we munch at mixed root-vegetable selections, and you find people knocking aside parsnip and celeriac to get at the ones in senatorial purple. In those days too we boiled beetroot in aluminium saucepans, having taken care to twist off the tops rather than cut them, as this would cause only mild bleeding rather than the full haemorrhage; now we roast them in a slow oven, no more than gas mark 1 or 2, and little blood escapes. In those days someone might, on a winter evening, have a go at bortsch; now it could be anything up to Simon Hopkinson's sophisticated and exquisite Jellied Beetroot Consommé with Sour Cream and Chives. You can scarcely toss a mixed green salad in a restaurant without discovering several leaves whose arteries and veins are purple. There is Beetroot Gratin and Beetroot Tarte Tatin. In defiance of Galen – who maintained that half-cooked beetroot 'leads to flatulence and stomach-ache, and it sometimes produces gripings' – there is a recipe for Beetroot Risotto, in which you cook half the raw shredded root from the start and add the other half near the end; this has always worked for me, and never sent anyone rushing for the gripe-water.

The French got there slightly before us. According to Elizabeth David, it was Pomiane who first broke down established prejudice against the vegetable. He was serving it hot with hare decades before Michel Guérard did so. He also mixed it (hot again) with cream and vinegar, 'a very un-French combination', notes David, 'and by no means the only one of his unconventional suggestions in the domain of vegetable cookery to arouse the scorn of reactionaries.'

But could beetroot have peaked? Having been rescued and then become fashionable, is it now a cliché? It certainly can be in the hands of the plate-decorator type of chef, where it is just a useful extra hue regardless of culinary relevance. Everything has its fashion cycle; even simple, necessary things. Take new potatoes: once we scraped them, then we left them unpeeled, then we sort of half-scrubbed them to leave artistically haphazard patches of skin; once we boiled them, then we stoved them, then we roasted them; and so on. Lesser staples move even more decisively in and out of fashion.

Perhaps beetroot is due to take a break, along with kiwi fruit and lemon grass and sun-dried tomatoes and lamb shanks. The consolation is that (unlike in times of war and famine, when we are reduced to 'roots of scarcity') something usually goes out only because something else has come in. Perhaps soon it will be the turn of pignuts, kohlrabi, Hamburg parsley and Jane Grigson's beloved seakale. And perhaps, one day, the French will even allow themselves to discover the parsnip.

NOT A DINNER PARTY

The restaurateur Kenneth Lo played Davis Cup tennis for China in the 1930s. The only time I met him, he was in his late seventies, but still treading the court. He told me his tennis had got better as he had entered his sixties. I asked him how, and why.

'More relaxed,' he replied.

It seemed odd at the time, but Wimbledon annually offers corroboration. Is there anything more anxious than the latest teenage hopeful, dripping with endorsements, driven on by a Tennis Mom or Pop, terrified of failure? Or anything finally more joyless than the supreme athleticism and robotic concentration necessary to make a champion? Victory often seems no more than an anguished release from defeat. And then, after the biffers and swatters and grunters have

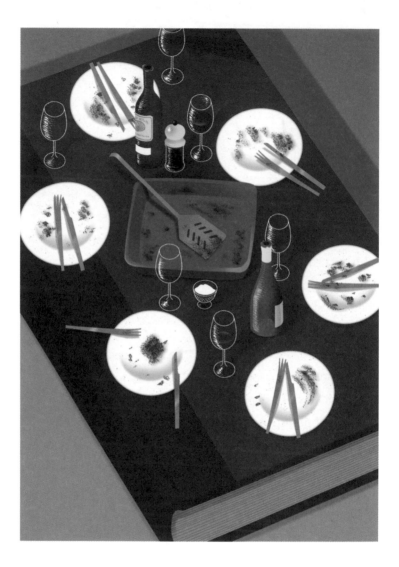

departed, a quartet of oldsters steps out into the evening sun, wiser brains atop slower muscles, evidently relaxed and enjoying the game as perhaps they haven't since childhood

At the time, I thought we were merely talking about tennis. But on reflection Lo's remark applies elsewhere, not least to his own field of food preparation. It ought, oughtn't it, to be all about pleasure? That of anticipation, as you plan and shop and cook; that of the act itself, as you eat among friends; afterwards, that of contented, not too self congratulatory remembering. But how rarely it turns out to be like this. All too often, high anxiety destroys the pleasures of anticipation, drink half-obliterates the moment itself, and the sort of hangover that makes it seem as if the washing-up keeps reproducing itself behind your back diminishes the recollection.

A few months ago, we had people to eat. One wife walked in, took a look at our table set for six, and said, 'How brave. I don't do dinner parties any more.'

To which the only reply was: 'This isn't a dinner party.'

For a start, because the phrase is banned in our household. Change the phrase and it does change your attitude. (I have a friend who once said wistfully, 'I might think about retiring if it wasn't called "retiring".') So 'friends are coming to supper' isn't a euphemism, just a different description. It doesn't mean you'll cook less assiduously or enjoy their company less – if anything, the contrary.

'A dinner party': what terrible words they are. Social duty as the ultimate Tennis Mom, with the domestic cook scrabbling along the baseline, convinced their backhand is just about to go to pieces under the pressure. And this pressure is subtly if unintentionally increased by food writers. A dinner party means you have to prepare three courses, doesn't it? Newspaper columns and cookbooks are frequently arranged so as to endorse this precept. Starter, main course, [cheese] in square brackets since at least you aren't expected to make that (or bake the biscuits), pudding. Seasonal menus, matched for you already, parts one, two, and three. The writer can do it, therefore you must and can too. And so you will, however much you inwardly protest: after all, you bought the book, didn't you?

Still, if the cookbooks are part of the problem, they can also come up with the solution. Step forward one of the heroes of my kitchen, Edouard de Pomiane. The first two pages of *Cooking with Pomiane* are headed 'The Duties of the Host' and might be expected to depress you. In fact they should be xeroxed and pasted to your extractor fan.

According to Pomiane, there are three kinds of guest who may invade your home:

(1) Those one is fond of.

(2) Those with whom one is obliged to mix.

(3) Those whom one detests.

For these graded occasions, 'One would prepare, respectively, an excellent dinner, a banal meal, or nothing at all, since in the latter case one would buy something ready cooked.' This is a useful distinction. It probably feels cheapskate and moralistic to work out in advance how much you like your guests; but is there anything more disheartening than cooking well for an unappreciative bore?

Of course, this still leaves you faced with preparing 'an excellent dinner' for 'those one is fond of'. Again, listen to Pomiane: 'For a successful dinner there should never be more than eight people. One should prepare *only one good dish.*' These are his italics, not mine. Don't they make the heart lift? It is still a three-course meal, or four with some square-bracketed cheese, but all the effort goes into the main course. And as Pomiane implies, you can always get something in from the *traiteur* or the *pâtissier* for either or both ends of the meal.

The French think nothing of this; and now that it's

relatively easy in this country to buy a range of decent hors d'oeuvres and a plausible fruit tart, there's no reason for us not to do the same. Argue it this way: which would your guests prefer: a host(ess) exhausted from having slaved until the last minute, or a livelier version of the same human being who has taken some entirely reasonable short-cuts? There is, doubtless, a residual puritanism to be overcome; and you must also subdue any sense that it's cheating to possibly half-misrepresent something from a shop as being your own creation. But it's only cheating if you actively claim that you did make it yourself.

Recently, with a crowded week and 'friends coming to supper', I remembered Pomiane's dictum, but played it the other way round. Instead of 'only one good dish', I went for two halves: the starter and pudding would come from my own hands; the main course, porcini lasagne, from the local Italian deli. The deal with the deli goes like this: you take along your own oven-to-table dish a couple of days in advance, then collect it filled and ready to cook. The presence of home-team tableware does, I admit, make it look sneakily as if you might have assembled the lasagne yourself.

The dinner – supper – went well and the chef was unstressed. No one said a word about my first course (mildly miffed) or for that matter my pudding (bastards). But everyone agreed: 'This lasagne is fantastic.'

'Good', I replied firmly. That seemed to cover it.

A fortnight later I got an e-mail from one of the guests – happily now abroad – repeating the praise and asking for the recipe. OK, so what would you have done? I looked up Marcella Hazan, listed what seemed the obvious ingredients, suggested a mix of fresh and dried porcini, and was utterly confident of the cooking time required (because the deli had told me). Again, that seemed to cover it. A week or so later, another e-mail: 'My lasagne wasn't half as good as yours.'

Even the wise Edouard de Pomiane has no advice about this situation.

BOTTOM DRAWER

Do you remember the old-fashioned mincing machine? The wing-nutted clamp that screwed on to the underside of the kitchen table; the curly spindle; the choice of tarnished metal nozzles; and the way the meat came out, leading the infant mind to dwell on murderers and victim-disposal? After a century or so, this trusty machine finally got a makeover; like other culinary fashion victims, I succumbed to one of those orange-and-white moulded-plastic jobs with a clever suction pad for making it stick – theoretically – to any surface. For some reason mine never worked; however much I spat on the rubber base to encourage the necessary vacuum, it was constantly toppling over as I wound the handle. So it went into the elephants' graveyard of discarded machinery, the *tiroir des refusés*, and I upgraded to a food processor. Since when mincing has become a thing of the past, and that old metal instrument as much of an antique as the brawn tin, the paste jagger, and the bread grater.

Yet I never managed to throw out my mincer that declined to clamp. It went from drawer to drawer, and finally to some limbo shelf alongside offcuts of matting and supernumerary bathroom tiles. While I have little trouble culling unwanted cookbooks, it always seems harder to discard implements. That bag of china heads which completely failed to hold down the pastry when I blind-baked; those bread tins acquired when my yeast fantasies were on the rise; that mortar whose pestle snapped in half and lingers on without its mate. I continue to hoard them, next to pots without lids (normal) and lids without pots (crazy).

In the Pedant's kitchen there is the usual drawer for knives and peelers and prodders, some 80 per cent of which see regular use. There's a large pot for wooden spoons, spatulas, and suchlike – 95 per cent use here, and it would be 100 per cent were it not for that inevitable large strainer-cum-spoon thing whose bowl is made from a gourd. But then there is the other drawer – the one where items of sporadic usefulness live, the one where everything is tangled up and furtive, into which you insert a tentative hand, not knowing where sharp edges lurk. When did I last empty it? Ten years ago? It seemed time to take an inventory.

It is a small drawer, but it disbursed eighty-two items (counting the pack of wooden barbecue skewers as one). The meat cleaver and the jelly bag see regular service; of the four champagne stoppers (I blame the generosity of friends), one is definitely used; and there's an egg-whisk and a turkey-baster which I have probably twirled and squirted at some point in the past decade. But the remainder? Inevitably, there's a pair of salad servers with giraffe handles; also a deeply unhygienic-looking white plastic spatula; there are twenty-one chopsticks; three knives and one fork from the days when airline cutlery seemed worth stealing; various adze-hewn wooden spoons, and a truffle-grater left by a guest; six comic bendy straws, a plasterer's tool 'which I must have thought handy for prising stuff off the barbecue', a deeply tarnished six-pronged serving fork of unknown origin and uncertain purpose, though fish is a possibility; and so on. Three assorted bits of ironmongery may or may not relate to the rotisserie we never used and junked years ago. At the very back of the drawer: one picture hook without its nail, two spider corpses, and a blanched almond.

With virile forcefulness I threw away the almond, the obscure metal bits and bobs, and the airline cutlery (it was so Eighties). Then I stalled. Logically, I could have discarded three of the four champagne stoppers, but each had a certain attraction. I did reduce the number of chopsticks, as cooking Chinese for ten-and-a-half people seemed improbable. For the rest, it was a case of throwing it all out or putting it all back. I put it all back.

This was a mixture of pathetic inertia and bound-to-come-in-useful culinary optimism. But it was also a sign and a promise to myself: one of these days the perfect kitchen will be attained and the final Judgment of Implements can be postponed until then. All cooks quarter-dream of this day. When we move into a new place, many of us make individualizing adjustments to the kitchen, but leave it largely as it is. Once in a lifetime, perhaps, we might tear the whole thing apart and plan it from the beginning. The Pedant and She For Whom He Cooks tried to do this about twenty years ago. We even consulted a design expert. We explained what we needed, then he explained what we needed; we discussed it, we dithered, we dithered some more, and one day he sacked us for terminal incertitude.

But you can't really know what you want until you've got

it wrong the first time. (Some apply that same principle to marriage.) There are people to help and advise, but even they have certain idées fixes. I once had a run-in with a kitchen fitter when I asked him to make the work surface on one side of the kitchen eight inches higher off the ground, for the perfectly sensible reason that I was eight inches taller than She For Whom. He didn't want to do that.

'Thirty four inches is the height of a work surface,' he repeated as an article of faith.

I in turn reprised what I wanted and why.

He fell into a silence, before coming up with what he judged a killer refutation. 'Ah, but what about when you sell the house?'

It's a comfort to know that even the most distinguished cooks don't always get what they want. The Wilder Shores of Gastronomy reprints Elizabeth David's description of her own Dream Kitchen. It would, she writes, be 'large, very light, very airy, calm and warm'; also, from the start, 'rigorously orderly'. There would be no 'unnecessary clutter', and all equipment and paraphernalia would be out of sight, except for items in constant use. So there would be a jar for wooden spoons – 'But half a dozen would be enough, not thirty-five as there are now'. You see: she's human, just like the rest of us. Though I somehow doubt any of those thirty-five spoons had giraffe handles.

Mrs David's kitchen would also have French windows, a double sink, a long continuous plate rack, two refrigerators, a chaise longue, two ovens, and a marble slab. The background colours would be cool: the only aubergine or tangerine would be provided by the real things. Gross errors typical of 'so-called modern kitchens' would be avoided. Amazingly, many are designed with 'refrigerators next to the cooking stove. This seems to me almost as mad as having a wine-rack above it.' The perfect Elizabeth David kitchen would, in summary, 'be more like a painter's studio furnished with cooking equipment than anything conventionally accepted as a kitchen'.

I read this description with some envy and a slight blush: yes, of course, the Pedant's refrigerator is right next to his oven. I just assumed the damn thing was properly insulated. And I was comforted, in a way, to learn that even Mrs David never had her fantasies quite fulfilled. Some time after describing her dream in print, she at last had a new kitchen installed in her Chelsea home, 'but the configuration of the house did not permit following her ideal plan'.

So it is with all our dreams. Perhaps I'll never get that

second oven I'm sure I need, let alone a Cornu range; nor will She For Whom get the wood-burning stove for which she occasionally pants. The kitchen will also continue to malfunction mildly; the sink will block, and various stuff – mainly fruit teas, fortunately – will carry on falling off the back of that too-clever-by-half corner swing drawer and go missing for months. But I shall attempt to see all this as a wider metaphor of culinary endeavour. Cooking is about making do with what you've got – equipment, ingredients, level of competence. It's a fallible procedure in which each small success needs praising, preferably more than it deserves. But imagine what things would be like if you actually got your dream kitchen. Your cooking would have to live up to it. Imagine the extra pressure that would impose. And if you botched a dish, there'd be no falling back on all those reliable old excuses. At least, thanks to Mrs David, I've now discovered a new one: 'I'm so sorry this didn't work out quite as it's meant to. But you see, some tosser put the fridge right next to the oven.'

THE MORAL OF IT ALL

On the second morning of the case brought by Oscar Wilde against the Marquess of Queensberry for criminal libel, there was a curious exchange between the defendant's counsel, Edward Carson, and the playwright. Carson was asking about Alfred Taylor, who had procured rent boys for Wilde, and whom Carson was seeking to establish as an evidently dubious character. For instance, he lived in the upper part of a house without a servant (and thus was not a gentleman); he had double curtains which were drawn even in daytime (aesthete); he burnt perfume in his rooms (worse than aesthete); he had young male friends, and so on. Including this:

CARSON: He used to do his own cooking?

WILDE: That I don't know. I have never dined with him there.

CARSON: Do you mean to say that you don't know that Taylor used to do his own cooking?

WILDE: No; nor if he did, should I think it anything wrong. I think it rather clever. You have asked me as a fact. I say I do not know, but I have never seen him, sir.

CARSON: I have not suggested that it is anything wrong.

WILDE: No, cooking is an art. (*Laughter*.)

CARSON: Another art?

WILDE: Another art.

Carson was, of course, certainly suggesting there might be something wrong. Put together with all the other stuff, the fact that a fellow was over-familiar with a frying-pan could be a clincher that he was not the full sovereign. And the laughter in court provoked by Wilde's innocuous description of cooking as an art suggests that Carson was well alive to the potential prejudices of an English jury.

Cooking is more usually seen as a morally neutral, if not actually positive endeavour; and cookery writing as even more free of Carsonesque aspersion. In 1923, Joseph

Conrad's wife, Jessie, published *A Handbook of Cookery for a Small House*. Her husband's preface begins like this:

> Of all the books produced since the remote ages by human talents and industry those only that treat of cooking are, from a moral point of view, above suspicion. The intention of every other piece of prose may be discussed and even mistrusted, but the purpose of a cookery book is one and unmistakable. Its object can conceivably be no other than to increase the happiness of mankind.

This is a grand statement, and properly uxorious, and we might well pass on convinced if Conrad did not promptly undermine his own authority with the following admission: 'I own that I find it impossible to read through a cookery book.' There are further caveats to be entered. For a start, we can imagine other examples of prose whose undoubted aim is to increase the happiness of mankind, from manuals of bee-keeping and relaxation technique to books about how to mend your own roof. Second, the notion that cookbooks are written from purer motives than other books is less clear now than in Conrad's day: watch the egomaniacal celebrity chef promoting the tie-in book of the TV series and you will witness worldly ambition as plainly as in any other area of personality publishing. And third, it is perfectly possible to think of a cookbook that would strike many people as actively immoral: one devoted, say, to ways of preparing the meat of endangered species.

But we know, essentially, what Conrad is saying. Here he is again: 'Good cooking is a moral agent.' Hmm, that word 'good': what exactly does he mean? 'By good cooking I mean the conscientious preparation of the simple food of everyday life, not the more or less skilful concoction of idle feasts and rare dishes.' We might catch a whiff of sturdy Puritanism, of tweed underpants, here. Presumably, if Mrs C. served Joseph a soft-boiled barnyard egg for his lunch with some home-baked bread, this would be good; whereas if, because it was his birthday, she went up to Fortnum & Mason, bought plovers' eggs and samphire and – I don't know – strewed the latter over the lightly poached former and served it with an olive ciabatta, this might qualify as a rare dish and thus bad?

It is at this point in his preface that Conrad's reasoning becomes a little wonkier. Sane cooking leads to good digestion, he says (true); and this, he argues, renders us cheerful and reasonable. As proof by counter-example, he adduces the diet of North American Indians.

The Noble Red Man was a mighty hunter, but his wives had not mastered the art of conscientious cookery – and the consequences were deplorable. The Seven Nations around the Great Lakes and the Horse tribes of the plains were but one vast prey to raging dyspepsia . . . [and] the domestic life of their wigwams was clouded by the morose irritability which follows the consumption of ill-cooked food.

This is what caused the 'unreasonable violence' of native Americans. As opposed, doubtless, to the reasonable violence of the British, French, Belgian, German and domestic American imperialists of the period, who ate so sensibly. The argument is like those that attribute national character to the weather or genius to illness – all-encompassing, unfalsifiable, yet manifestly bonkers. Abbé Prevost, the author of *Manon Lescaut*, thought the British predilection for suicide could be explained by their consumption of half-cooked beef (as well as by coal fires and too much sex). We might as well suggest that current American military zeal is a consequence of that nation's love of fast food – in which case, an infantryman's widow would probably have a lawsuit against the nearest burger outlet. And if anyone is tempted to believe in an automatic link between protein and aggression, don't forget that Hitler was a vegetarian.

Still, we continue to know and approve what Conrad is advocating: simplicity; conscientiousness; eating to live rather than living to eat. At the gastric heart of many of us there lingers a rural fantasy of self-sufficiency: that little cottage in a sheltered valley with a vegetable patch and some chickens, where you would live and eat according to the true cycle of the seasons, digging, planting, harvesting, cooking, consuming; producing enough for your own needs and a small surplus for barter. It could still be done, more or less, in Conrad's day. His great friend Ford Madox Ford had just such a life in West Sussex after the First World War. He shared a cottage called Red Ford with the Australian painter Stella Bowen, and wrote about the experience with both lyricism and unsentimentality. They had a goat and a pig, and a boy to help with the digging, and – Ford being Ford – there were grand, madcap schemes way beyond his capabilities: one was to breed disease-free potatoes, another to discover 'the philosopher's stone of agriculture', a method of 'wastelessly administering nutriment to plants'.

He was also lord of the kitchen. In her autobiography, *Drawn from Life*, Bowen described Ford as 'one of the great cooks'. He was also 'utterly reckless with the butter and reduced the kitchen to the completest chaos. When he cooked, one kitchen-maid was hardly sufficient to wait upon him. But he did not mind how much trouble he took, and he never wasted scraps. Every shred of fat was rendered down, and every cabbage stalk went into the stock-pot which stood eternally on the living-room fire.'

Ford carried on cooking for the rest of his life. On the eve of the next world war, after a literary conference in Boulder, Colorado, he cooked *Chevreuil des prés salés* as a farewell supper. Among those present was the twenty-year-old Robert Lowell. A quarter of a century later, Lowell called it 'the best dinner he had ever had'. Ford being a great novelist, there was also a serious element of fiction about his preparations. 'You never realized,' Lowell added, 'that the venison was mutton that Ford had cooked.'

Philip Larkin believed that 'Poetry is an affair of sanity', as opposed to what he called (after a phrase from Evelyn Waugh) the 'very mad, very holy' school. Cooking too is an affair of sanity – even literally so. Stella Bowen once knew a poet in Montparnasse who had suffered a nervous breakdown and been incarcerated in a clinic. After his release, he lived in a room overlooking a street in which there was a *boulangerie*. The poet dated his recovery from the moment when, gazing out of his window, he saw a woman going in to buy bread. He felt, he told Bowen, 'unutterably envious of the interest she was taking in the choosing of a loaf'.

That's what it's about. You choose a loaf. You are reckless with the butter. You reduce the kitchen to chaos. You try not to waste scraps. You feed your friends and family. You sit around a table engaged in the irreducible social act of sharing food with others. For all the cavils and caveats, Conrad was right. It is a moral act. It is an affair of sanity. Let him have the last word. 'The intimate influence of conscientious cookery,' he wrote, 'promotes the serenity of mind, the graciousness of thought, and that indulgent view of our neighbour's failings which is the only genuine form of optimism. Those are its titles to our reverence.'

Actually, I've one or two cavils about this, too, but – there's something boiling over. I must go. I have an idle feast to prepare.